THE "LAST DAYS" ARE BEHIND US:
OUR BEST DAYS ARE AHEAD!

An Antidote for Alarmist End-Time Viewpoints and a Biblical Proposal for a Positive Future

JERRY TRITLE

MDiv, MBA, BA

With love and gratitude to Jennifer.

Jennifer Tritle holds a Master's of Science in Clinical/Counseling Psychology and a Bachelor of Arts in Psychology. She's worked as a therapist specializing in sexual abuse victims, especially children and has taught psychology courses in various subject areas at the university level. She is an artist, writer, and editor, as well as principle in her business, "Passages." She has been published in art, literary, and theological trade magazines and journals. Jennifer homeschooled her children for nearly a decade, and her deepest passions are her family and home. She has collaborated with her husband Jerry of nearly 35 years on published topics of theology and life.

ISBN: 979-8-35091-462-7 paperback
ISBN: 979-8-35091-463-4 ebook

TABLE OF CONTENTS

TABLES

NO, WE'RE NOT LIVING IN THE LAST DAYS. THIS IS NOT THE END OF THE WORLD.

Why wouldn't a rational person, especially a Bible-believing Christian, think that these are the Last Days and the End of the world when taking a gaze at the world around us? After all, Jesus did say, "Take heed that no one deceives you…you will hear of wars and rumors of wars. See that you are not troubled; for all these things must come to pass, but the end is not yet. For nation will rise against nation, and kingdom against kingdom. And there will be famines, pestilences, and earthquakes in various places."[1] These types of events, as recorded in Matthew's Gospel, have moved devout Christians throughout history when the world around them was seemingly in chaos to believe that the Last Days were upon them. And although having believed those Last Days about which Jesus spoke were upon them, the fact is, the "end" of the world, as most interpret it, has not yet come. Fifth century Church Father Andrew of Caesarea, in contrast, wrote a commentary on the Revelation of Jesus Christ during a time when the falling Roman Empire was confronting bubonic plague, civil war, famine, and catastrophic Persian invasions. Andrew, the Archbishop of Caesarea, did not presume to think that the "coming of the Lord" was near when he wrote that commentary. He did not view the Book of Revelation as a contemporary doomsday scenario, but instead described it as a "useful, God-inspired" book that would "guide those who read it to a blessed end."[2]

So, the question remains, "When will the last days to which Jesus referred be?" How long will they go on? And has anyone ever asked the question, "Last

---

[1] Matt 24:4-7.

[2] Constantinou, Eugenia Scarvelis: <u>Guiding to a Blessed End</u>: Andrew of Caesarea & His Apocalypse Commentary in the Ancient Church.

days of what?" If the end of the world and time as we know it is near and upon us now today, how can we nurture any Bible-based hope of building a family, an estate, a church, a nation, or have any hope for the future at all?

Focusing on world events without having a biblical framework by which to interpret them can certainly lead to a "Last Days" obsession by Christians and non-Christians alike and lead to what some refer to as "Last Days madness." This frenzy quenches human hope for the victory of righteousness, peace, justice, and joy in the future promised in Scripture because of the work of Jesus Christ on the cross. This Last Days madness overrides the faith of those who pray, "Thy Kingdom come," and is exacerbated not only by faulty theologies and their resultant pessimism, fear of death, and worry of impending doom, on the part of their hearers, but also by the calamity-filled messages from global leaders in politics, economics, science, and education. Many in these realms proclaim immanent apocalypse if their prescribed political agendas are not approved. Yet, time has proven these forecasts of apocalyptic events false.

The recent 2023, World Economic Forum gathered in Davos, Switzerland, exemplifies this threatening of humanity. It focused on the world's doom and immanent collapse associated with wars, unsubstantiated man-made climate disasters, the myth of overpopulation, energy price chaos, inflation, epidemics of hunger and disease, political instability, and widening economic inequity. They propose a New World Order as the only means of warding off these calamities. Christians and non-Christians alike allow panic to grip their hearts based on their hearing these types of messages. They succumb to these false views of the present and the future because they have no biblical foundation in Christ's Lordship and the growing nature of His Kingdom of righteousness, peace, and joy filling the earth today. The two world wars of the twentieth century and the evil associated with them marked the beginning of a time when many churches abandoned their teaching of that hope of seeing God's Kingdom expand throughout the earth, thus reserving the rule of God's domain to heaven alone. Due to unbelief in the victory of the Gospel message, Last Days adherents tend to grow in greater faith in the power of the devil and evil men and their organizations taking over the earth than in faith in the greater power of the resurrected and reigning Christ. That error focuses on a world falling apart until the End.

Not knowing history or a biblical theology regarding the End, many erroneously believe we are now living in the Last Days, the Antichrist is coming, those not saved will be marked in some way with the Mark of the Beast, and they will either go through a Great Tribulation or partake of the "Rapture of the Church." Thinking that they are in a particular dispensation of time versus seeing themselves as part of a timeline of continuity spreading from the Old Testament through the New Testament through now, they err. They forget that all of the enemies of God (e.g., Pharaoh of Egypt, Nebuchadnezzar of Babylon, Cyrus of Persia, Antiochus Epiphanes of Greece, and Caesar Nero of Rome) and all of their kingdoms are now but dust and have been all but forgotten, and that these powers were much more powerful in the world in their times than that of Hitler, Stalin, or al Qaeda leader Osama bin Laden ever were or ever could be in ours. Believing these errors, many Christians regard bringing heaven to this world as a cynical pipe dream, saying that those who preach the Gospel of God's victorious Kingdom is likened unto "polishing the brass on a sinking ship." It is erroneous to think that the earth has been permanently placed in Satan's hand and is doomed until Jesus reigns over it at His "Second Coming." The "rapture," a contemporary teaching of dispensational churches who believe in a secret snatching away of the Church prior to a Great Tribulation to come, is a hope of escape to many who fear a current apocalypse. Yet, the Lord never promised to take the Church out of this world's calamities and tribulation. Instead, Jesus Christ has been reigning since the first century when He said that all authority on heaven and earth were His and that His disciples were to go into the nations, discipling them and teaching them to observe all His commandments. No comfort, in this writer's opinion, can be gained from the doctrine of the rapture prior to, during, or after a supposedly future Great Tribulation. As a matter of fact, at present these doctrines about the timing of the Great Tribulation in regard to the rapture introduce further fights and contention among believers already fearful of the end. These pessimistic and recent teachings were introduced to the world by religious sects like the Millerites of the early 1800s, who taught during chaotic world events of that time that Jesus' return was imminent. **Note that!** In 1800 years of Church history, no such doctrines existed. Merely 200 years old, and they now grip our minds as if they are Absolute Truth. Jesus' words about conditions at the time of His coming were right and true, but, we are missing the point if we think He was talking about events of any time in history other than that very first century in which He lived, as we will attempt to prove here. The current escapist teaching of the rapture has done well to infiltrate most Christian fundamentalists and modern evangelical churches, especially after the doctrine was formally documented within the Dake's Study and Schofield Reference bibles. Prior to this time, the Church had never embraced such a teaching as part of its doctrine of last things. Today, the doctrine of the rapture and the imminent return of Jesus Christ are standard teachings within the dispensational school of eschatology in many church denominations and even now in some mainline churches. This instruction causes stumbling with regard to the true nature of Christ's Lordship and the power of His Kingdom, which is now filling the earth victoriously as the prophets of old and Jesus and His apostles made clear. As was mentioned, the most powerful kingdoms and rulers that the world has ever known are no more, and the Church and Her words of Christ the King have been covering the earth successfully for two millennia and will continue to do so.

Believing that a rapture is immanent, that we're living in the Last Days with the end of time being near, and that the Great Tribulation is upon us, negates the truth that Jesus Christ began His actual reign when He stated that all authority in heaven, and on earth, and under the earth was His.[3] These beliefs also deny belief in Jesus' words that the time of His coming and the coming of His Kingdom in power was at hand *at the time of His ministry on earth* and that He was *coming quickly* upon the *first century world*. If this were not the case, Jesus' message to His first century audience would have been irrelevant. Finally, it should be noted that these contemporary belief systems do not think it plausible that every word Jesus spoke about tribulation and the desolation of Jerusalem came to pass in A.D. 70. The events delineated in Matthew, Chapters 23-24, came to pass word-for-word in A.D. 70, affirming Jesus' prophecies against unbelieving Jerusalem and her then corrupt rulers. All of these things did come to pass during the lifespan of that first century terminal generation that would see the end of the Great Tribulation in A.D. 66-70.

---

[3] Matt 28: 18-20; c.f., Phil 2:9-11.

Some would ask, how can you be sure the Last Days are behind us and that the Lord came in A.D. 70, when even Jesus Himself said that He did not know the day or the hour of His return? Good question. Jesus Christ was neither ambiguous nor ignorant about the Last Days; however, there seems to me to have been a time when He received full knowledge of His return to restore the Kingdom to the New Israel, that also being the time when He received the Revelation of Jesus Christ (the Book of Revelation) from His Father. Until He received that Revelation of Himself from the Father, Jesus as fully man, yet fully God in the Second Person, knew neither the day nor the hour of His coming upon Jerusalem. The Revelation of Jesus Christ, given to the Apostle John on the Isle of Patmos, represented the sealing of God's vision and prophecy to both Christ and His people according to Daniel the prophet.[4] As a twenty-first century believer researching the complete, or sealed, canon of Sacred Scripture of both the Old and New Testaments; relying on the historic Church's dogmas, doctrines, and teachings; and assessing the covenantal events that have occurred in history itself, such as the Destruction of Jerusalem in A.D. 70, a fulfillment of Jesus' words in passages like Matthew 24, I propose a conclusion embraced by many theologians and Christians throughout history that state that it is profoundly clear that the "Last Days" of Old Covenant Israel and Jerusalem, as well as the coming of the Lord Jesus to inaugurate His Kingdom in power, occurred in the first century. That was the time of that *"end of the age"* about which the disciples were asking in Matthew Chapter 24. Furthermore, other "end of the age" events, such as the binding of Satan and the *beginning* of the Thousand-Year Reign of Christ also happened in the first century. In fact, the Kingdom of God under the Lordship of Jesus Christ has been filling the earth since then, and the Word of the Lord has been covering it as the prophets have declared since the Old Covenant economy was "shaken" out of the way.[5]

God the Father told His Son Jesus upon His Ascension to the throne of the Kingdom of God in A.D. 30, "Sit here at my right hand until I make all

---

[4] See Table 2: Daniel's 70 Weeks Prophecy.

[5] Heb 12:26-28.

of Your enemies a footstool for Your feet."[6] This often quoted Old Testament passage in the New Testament clearly tell us that our Lord Jesus Christ was not only enthroned during the first century, but that He also remains in the heavens reigning from His throne and will not "return to judge the living and the dead" until His Father subdues under foot all who oppose His Son's dominion in this world. Our Lord reigns *now*. This has been the continuing cause for the Church's praise and worship of Christ the King throughout the past 2000 years of history, unchallenged until recent times. Belief in the reign of our Savior and King Jesus, the Christ, is the essence of the Gospel of the Kingdom of God that Christ and His apostle's preached. Jesus and the Kingdom of God was and is the preached message that confronted the kings and kingdoms of this world and that subsequently caused martyrdom and great Church growth from the first century on. That truthful message saves us from the paralyzing fears of pending, looming Great Tribulation to come and the panicked hoping for an immanent rapture to escape this world's uncertainties and chaos. Seeing those last days of Jerusalem as rightly behind us frees us from the pessimistic and faulty theology and doomsday messages that take us away from our calling to bring heaven to earth in all things and in all areas of life. This is accomplished through the preaching of the Gospel of the Kingdom, while trusting in the Spirit of God's work to change and redeem mankind and the creation itself. Mankind discipled in that change brings about God's Kingdom on earth as it is in heaven.

The truth is that Jesus Christ began His reign 2000 years ago. He has reigned since then, and His reign continues powerfully today. Christ's Kingdom is filling the earth in THESE days. Christ's Kingdom is conquering and growing as a sort of "mop-up" action after His Kingdom came in A.D. 70. After He bound the devil after the first century Great Tribulation, loud voices in heaven declared definitively that "the kingdoms of this world BECAME the kingdoms of our God and of His Christ."[7] As a result, we have seen and will progressively see more blessings and prosperity in the earth now and in the future based on Christ's first century finished redemptive works and His continuing works as Lord over the

---

[6] Ps(s) 110:1; Matt 22:34; Mark 12:36; Luke 20:43; Heb 1:13; 10:13.

[7] Rev 11:15.

earth. Because Jesus bound Satan then, we only need now to believe in the work of Christ and His forgiveness of our sins, obey His Commandments, and prevail against the gates of hell in Jesus' Name as we walk in His power.

Be of good cheer, the last days are behind us and our best days as a Church are ahead. I should state that to reject the rapture theory, or to say that we are not living in the Last Days, are certainly not new theological inventions by any means. Furthermore, I am not saying that those who hold those views are not Christian. They are my brethren; however, I, along with many throughout the past two millennia have a different view of last things. The excellent sources listed in the back of this book present but a few of the works touching this topic that affirm whole or in part that belief system. Most Orthodox and Catholic churches hold to the truth that Christ is King and reigning now and that the Church is living in the Thousand-Year Reign, referred to often as the Millennial Reign of Christ. In honor of this truth, the Catholic Church annually celebrates Christ the King Sunday at the conclusion of every liturgical year.[8] Sadly, many who hold that Christ is currently reigning, however, only see His reign as being effectual in heaven and not the earth. As a result, the effects of that particular interpretation of Christ's reign are just as impotent a message to this world as that of the escapist doctrines. Both teachings malnourish the Church's Spirit-filled stamina and optimism to preach the Gospel in power and with faith that God

---

[8] Quas Primas, the ENCYCLICAL OF POPE PIUS XI ON THE FEAST OF CHRIST THE KING: "His empire includes not only Catholic nations, not only baptized persons…but also all those who are outside the Christian faith; so that truly the whole of mankind is subject to the power of Jesus Christ. Nor is there any difference in this matter between the individual and the family or the State; for all men, whether collectively or individually, are under the dominion of Christ. In him is the salvation of the individual, in him is the salvation of society…He is the author of happiness and true prosperity for every man and for every nation…If, therefore, the rulers of nations wish to preserve their authority, to promote and increase the prosperity of their countries, they will not neglect the public duty of reverence and obedience to the rule of Christ. What We said at the beginning of Our Pontificate concerning the decline of public authority, and the lack of respect for the same, is equally true at the present day. "With God and Jesus Christ excluded from political life, with authority derived not from God but from man, the very basis of that [human] authority has been taken away, because the chief reason of the distinction between ruler and subject has been eliminated. The result is that human society is tottering to its fall, because it has no longer a secure and solid foundation."

will change individuals, families, and nations to embrace God's Savior, Christ Jesus, and to press His crown rights into every realm of life. Doing so will also sanctify the creation which longs for such a salvation.[9]

To speak about the Last Days by necessity requires a discussion about the Kingdom of God and how it has had many comings in history. We see these comings of the Lord in judgment upon His enemies to save His people[10] in the cases of Egypt,[11] Nineveh,[12] and in His coming in judgment upon Jerusalem to establish His Church as His new kingdom in AD 70.[13] We also see Christ's coming on the last day of human history after all of Christ's enemies are made a footstool for His feet, referred to as Christ's Second Coming.[14] So, throughout redemptive history, since the Garden of Eden and mankind's fall, the Kingdom has come many times as will be shown. It is apropos that God's Kingdom, the presence of His rule and reign, comes throughout history. It is the answer to the prayer, "Thy Kingdom Come. Thy will be done on earth as it is in heaven."

When we pray, "Thy Kingdom come," do we believe that heaven's will would be accomplished in every realm of earth, including the lives of rulers, families, and nations? Do we even know what we're praying for when we pray such a petition? We are not merely praying for the end of the world and our going to heaven while the earth falls apart behind us. On the contrary, as the fathers of the faith have said about this second petition in the Lord's prayer, we are praying for God's sovereign rule over our lives here on earth every day we live. We submit to His authority and yield to His control in every aspect of our existence so that God's sovereign rule will come now and in the future in its fullness and permanence. With the Lord's Prayer, the Church has also prayed prayers associated with

---

[9] Rom 8:18-22.

[10] Ps(s) 18:8-14.

[11] Isa 19:1, Eze 32:7-8.

[12] Nah. 1:1-11.

[13] Matt 24:30, Acts 2:19-21, Rev 1:7.

[14] 1 Cor 15:20-28; Rev 20:9.

the Kingdom from Scripture, such as prayers of praise and adoration to God,[15] imprecatory prayers for God's overthrow of our enemies,[16] prayers of confession and repentance from sin,[17] prayers of intercession for the Church,[18] and prayers for salvation and deliverance.[19] God commands we pray these prayers in faith if we want answers. St. James taught us to "…ask in faith, nothing doubting… for he who doubts is like a wave of the sea driven and tossed by the wind. For let not that man suppose that he will receive anything from the Lord."[20] Jesus said, "…and whatever things you ask in prayer, believing, you will receive." The writer of the Epistle to the Hebrews stated, "For without faith, it is impossible to please God.[21]

A final note on the coming of the Kingdom: the Kingdom of God comes definitively, progressively, and then finally. For example, in Jesus' parable of the mustard seed, we see that the Kingdom of God comes in Christ Jesus, which *is a definitive* presence of the Kingdom among men. The Kingdom expands *progressively* in the earth to this day. *Finally*, the Kingdom of God will come in its consummate and final form at the end of Christ's Thousand-Year Reign as He comes one last time to judge the living and the dead. The late Pope Benedict XVI gives us both a timely and timeless insight into how the Kingdom's coming affects heaven AND earth. He stated, "Praying fervently for the coming of the Kingdom also means being constantly alert for the signs of its presence and working for its growth in every sector of society. It means facing the challenges of present and future with confidence in Christ's victory and a commitment to extending His reign. It means not losing heart in the face of resistance, adversity, and scandal. It means overcoming every separation between faith and life and countering heresy. It also means rejecting the false dichotomy between faith and

---

[15] E.g., praying Ps(s) 48.

[16] E.g., praying Ps(s) 7; 35; 58; 59; 69; 83; 109; 137; 139.

[17] E.g., praying Ps(s) 51.

[18] E.g., praying Ps(s) 51:18; 74.

[19] E.g., praying Ps(s) 6; 20; 22; 28.

[20] James 1:5-7.

[21] Heb 11:6.

political life, since, as the Second Vatican Council put it, "there is no human activity—even in secular affairs—which can be withdrawn from God's dominion." The Council also stated, "It means working to enrich . . . society and culture with the beauty and truth of the Gospel, and never losing sight of that great hope which gives meaning and value to all the other hopes which inspire our lives."[22]

To truly understand where the Last Days fall within the timeline of history, one needs to examine the history of God's relationship to mankind from the Garden of Eden prior to the Fall of Adam through the final coming of Christ to judge the living and the dead at the end of Christ's current reign. This time frame is referred to as "redemptive history." We need to go back to the beginning in Eden because that is where God gave mankind through Adam His order; that is, His cultural mandate to mankind through Adam to be fruitful, fill the earth, and dominate it for the glory of God. After Adam's fall into sin, God enacted a Covenant of Grace between Himself and mankind that would unfold ever more deeply and powerfully through history. The timelines in this book depict the deeper cuts of that Covenant of Grace that have occurred since the Garden, including the Old and the New Covenants. When we examine redemptive history in terms of a continuity of the Covenant of Grace with Old Testament Israel and New Testament Israel, which is the Church, we can see where the Last Days lie at the end of the First Covenant.

This book establishes the biblical reasons for an eschatology of hope and victory based on rightly understanding the implications of the reign of Christ Jesus and the current expansion of His Kingdom. Fourth century Church father Athanasius I of Egypt understood the triumphant nature of the Lord's reign better than most throughout history, as was attested to by his saying, "The Lord calls his ransomed people to sing songs of victory." This victory provides us with a robust Christian life as we work, and as we enjoy our friends, marriages, families, Church, and nation. Our believing and living the victorious truth that Jesus Christ is the reigning King and Lord, and that the Church's mission is to feed and tend the growing flock of believers as the nations are discipled over time (i.e., are "Christianized") brings us an anchored assurance to one's life and good works.

---

[22] Pope Benedict XVI, <u>Thy Kingdom Come, Jesus of Nazareth</u>.

Here are a few quick answers to some of the most frequently asked questions about the Last Days, which I will expound upon in the upcoming five charts and six chronological timelines in this book:

Are We Living in the Last Days?

No, we are not. The Last Days refer to the last days of the first covenant between God and His people made at Mount Sinai and administrated by Moses, as shown in Table 4. The disciples of Jesus wanted to know from Him when the end of *that* "age," not the "world," would come to pass. Many Bible translations of that famous passage in Matt 24:3 erroneously translate the Greek word *aeon* as "world" instead of "age," and this exacerbates the confusion. The world is NOT going to be destroyed, for then there would be nothing for the meek to inherit.[23] The disciples were asking about the time of the end of the Old Covenant Age when the city and the temple would be "left desolate without one stone remaining on top of another," which occurred with the destruction of Jerusalem in A.D. 70. We will show the prophecies as well as the fulfillment of these Last Days in Tables 2, 3, and 4, which also address the prophet Daniel's 70 Weeks prophecy, which clearly depicts the last days of Daniel's people, national Israel, which ended on the 1st of the month of Tishri, A.D. 70.

When Did Christ's Reign Begin? Is Christ Really Reigning Today?

Although Jesus was born a King *circa* (*c.*) 4 B.C., He went forth preaching the Gospel of the Kingdom of God as King of that Kingdom in A.D. 26. Recall that He affirmed to Pontius Pilate that He was a King and that His Kingdom did not have its origins in this world, but had its source from heaven itself.[24] In A.D.

---

[23] Matt 5:5.

[24] Matt 27:11.

30, however, sometime after Jesus' Resurrection and before His final Ascension to heaven, which occurred 40 days after His Resurrection, He ascended to His Father to receive His Kingdom, His coronation, and to sit at His Father's right hand "until all of His enemies were made a footstool for His feet." His reign over heaven, earth, and under the earth began at that coronation in heaven in A.D. 30.[25] This is why His disciples were said to have preached "another King" (Jesus). Affirming publicly that there was another King other than Caesar caused the Roman rulers and the rulers of the Jews great angst.[26] Then, as promised, and as expected by the apostles and disciples, Jesus Christ and His Kingdom came in power in A.D. 70, a sign of which was the destruction of Jerusalem and its temple.[27] Jesus' disciples knew this and warned the Jews and the Gentiles of the immanent coming of the Lord Jesus and His Kingdom, also known as His Appearing, or His Parousia as we shall learn. Christ's coming to establish His Kingdom brought with it His salvation for His people, the Church, and His vengeance against those among the Jews who had apostatized and were persecutors of His Church.[28] That powerful coming of the Lord and His Kingdom

---

[25] Dan 7:13-14.

[26] Acts 17:7.

[27] Matt 23:38; 24:3, 29-31.

[28] When the term "apostate" or "apostasy" is used in this work pertaining to the majority of Jewish rulers and a large portion of the Jewish people living in the provinces of the Roman Empire, and particularly in Jerusalem, in the first century A.D., this author is not engaging in careless or bigoted antisemitism. This work is written humbly regarding the first century Jewish nation's encounter with Jesus, the Christ of both Jews and Gentiles. One must remember that our Christianity has as its root the faith of Abraham, Moses, and the believing children of Israel, all of which supports the salvation of all of us outside of Israel through Christ. The apostasy of many of the Jews turned out for the salvation of the Gentiles, for St. Paul turned to the Gentiles with the Gospel once he was rejected by the Jews (Acts 13:46). We all were sinners with the proclivity to sin, and we remember the Psalmist who said in Psalm 130:3, "If You, Lord, should mark iniquities, O Lord, who could stand? But there is forgiveness with You, that You may be feared." So, these conclusions are not those of an antisemite, but of one who wants to portray the covenantal truths of the ending of one covenant and the beginning of the new as it pertains not only to the former Jewish nation and its Great City of Jerusalem, but also to the whole world. This author recognizes and esteems the Jewish fathers of the Christian faith and understands the sense of mourning seen in Jesus and in His apostles regarding the Jewish nation's rejection of their Christ and the ramifications of that rejection in the first century. Jesus seemingly mourns over Jerusalem, as recorded in Matt 23:37-39,

came quickly on that day in A.D. 70, as manifested in the fall of the Great City of Jerusalem and its temple, which was seen by all as that expected "appearing" of the Lord. This was the event that was a sign of the Son of Man reigning in heaven. That first century event was the beginning of Christ's reign. Within that event was the establishment of the Church as the New Jerusalem (for she had persevered through the Great Tribulation between A.D. 66-70), and the inauguration of the New Heavens and New Earth.[29] From that day forward, the 1st of Tishri, in A.D. 70, the Kingdom of God has been powerfully filling the earth. It took

---

longing that they would have turned to God through His message. He saw the impending doom destined for the house of Israel and that unbelieving generation. St. Paul, also a Jew, wrote in Rom 9:1-5 that he was sorrowful in heart and filled with grief over the Jews' rejection of the Gospel of Jesus Christ, adding that he wished that he were accursed from God if such a judgment were to bring to his countrymen a faith in Christ's salvation. Jesus and Paul both knew that the house of Israel would bear the brunt of God's wrath for their rejection of the Christ. Many Christian writers on the topic of the coming of Christ and the Kingdom of God recognize clearly and nearly unanimously that Jesus and His apostles, including St. Peter and St. Paul, categorized many of the Jews, and especially their rulers as having apostatized from the historic and orthodox faith of Abraham and Moses. Jesus, Himself, referred to His generation of Jews living at the time of His ministry as a faithless and perverse generation, as did the prophet Jeremiah prior to the judgment of Babylonian captivity in the sixth century B.C. Jesus also referred to the rulers of the Jews in Jerusalem, the Scribes and Pharisees, as hypocrites, broods of vipers, perverted from the faith, and those upon whom the fierce wrath and judgment of God would come for their apostasy and for their causing the whole nation to stumble and reject Jesus as Christ. Very harsh words from the God-man. It should be noted that the Gospel of the Kingdom of God was to the Jews first and then to the Gentiles. Many of the Jews believed and were baptized into Christ; however, the rest, the unbelievers who rejected in heart and deeds the faith of their father Abraham, bore the wrath of God in A.D. 70, with the destruction of Jerusalem and its temple. St. Peter and St. John told the Jews in Jerusalem that they and their rulers murdered Jesus the Christ "in ignorance," not seeing the salvation of God before them. The message to the Jews today as was made by Jesus and the apostles in the first century, is that God now commands all men everywhere to repent of unbelief and to believe on Jesus Christ as Yahweh, Messiah, Lord, King, and Savior of all the world (See Acts 17:29-31). This book attempts to portray truthfully and with charity the association between the Jews and the Last Days and Kingdom of God as depicted in Sacred Scripture.

[29] Rev 19 presents the end of the Great Tribulation with the Appearing of Christ on the White Horse (Christ's Parousia), which is the end of the second major vision in the Revelation. Rev 21:1-3 depicts what also occurs at His Appearing: the inauguration of the New Heavens and New Earth, and the Church displayed as the New Jerusalem. We see the same depiction recorded in 2 Pet 3:1-14.

only 300 years for the Kingdom of Christ to fill the Roman Empire and for its people to look to the Church for salvation during and after the Roman Empire's downfall as the prophet Daniel had predicted. Today, there is not a square mile on earth that is not under the authority of a Church diocese and bishop. So yes, Christ is really reigning today.

Was the Lord's Coming in A.D. 70, the Second Coming?

No, not as the Church understands the term "Second Coming." There will indeed be a final coming, or as it has been termed, "a second coming" of the Lord Jesus to judge the living and the dead. The Scriptures and the dogmatic theological statements of the Church agree that there will be a final coming again of Christ Jesus on the last day of human history.[30] This coming of the Lord will occur after Christ's current Thousand-Year Reign expires, which will occur when, and only when, as it is written, all of Christ's enemies are made a footstool for His feet, thus making way for the Final Judgment of the living and the dead.[31] What happened in A.D. 70 was the coming of the Lord's Kingdom in power as He had promised his disciples.[32] This was *a* coming, also referred to as an *appearing* that He promised would happen before all of His disciples would die. This coming of our Lord came to pass, in which He saved His Church, and exacted vengeance upon the apostasy of Jerusalem while St. John was still alive, as St. Irenaeus recorded.[33] This coming of the Lord was referred to in the Gospels as the "coming of the Son of Man," "the sign of the Son of Man in heaven," and "the sign of Christ's coming," about which the disciples inquired in the same sentence as when they inquired about the end of the age.[34] The word "coming" in the phrase "coming of the Lord" in this context is the Greek word *Parousia*,

---

[30] The Apostles Creed; the Nicene Creed; the Catechism of the Catholic Church, Article VII.

[31] Ps(s) 110:1; Matt 22:44; Mark 12:36; Luke 20:42; Acts 2:34; Heb 1:13.

[32] Matt 16:28; Mark 9:1; Luke 9:27. St. John lived to see the Coming of the Lord in A.D. 70.

[33] Gentry, The Beast of the Revelation, page 151, quoting: Coxe, Ante-Nicene Fathers 1:559-560.

[34] Matthew 24:3, 37, 39

which means "coming," "presence," or "active presence." The sense of this word is that the Lord was actively present at the Fall of Jerusalem *but was not literally seen*. The events that occurred at Christ's Parousia that could be seen with the naked eye were the outward manifestations of His invisible presence: Jerusalem's fall, the temple's being burned to the ground, the Jews who remained in the city being taken captive, the temple furniture being hauled away to Rome, and the abrogation of the entire Old Testament economy and redemptive system. These happenings were clear evidences that the Lord Jesus was directing the destruction of the city and its temple from His throne in heaven. This Parousia of the Lord in A.D. 70, was NOT His Second Coming (as is commonly referred to by the Church), which will occur at the end of Christ's current Thousand-Year Reign. Again, after Christ's reign expires, He will return to judge the living and the dead, throw death and Hades into the Lake of Fire, and then forever live within His elect and glorified people forever.

What Is the Thousand-Year Reign of Christ? Are We Living in It?

Throughout Sacred Scripture, the phrase "a thousand years" is used symbolically in both ancient Hebrew and Ancient Greek numerology to denote "fullness," as in a fullness of time or as to fullness of a quantity. This Thousand-Year Reign of Christ is not a literal one-thousand-year period, but a period that lasts from the destruction of Jerusalem until the time, however specifically God wills to define it, when all of Christ's enemies are made a footstool for His feet.[35] Therefore, Christ's Thousand-Year Reign could be thousands of years, but it is the ONE reign of Christ. "Fullness" is the important component of the definition, just as "fullness" is the sense when the psalmist states that God owns the cattle on a thousand hills. God owns them all. Moreover, as St. Peter has said, as to the Lord, "a day is as a thousand years, and a thousand years as a day."[36]

---

[35] Ps(s) 110:1; Matt 22:44; Mark 12:36; Luke 20:43; Acts 2:35; Heb 1:13; 10:13; c.f., Rev 20-22; Isa 2, and Mic. 4.

[36] Ps(s) 50:10; 2 Pet 3:8.

The blessings on earth as Christ's reign continues will be apparent even to the extent that, through the preaching of the Gospel of the Kingdom of Christ's reign and Lordship, nations will ultimately beat their weapons of war into implements of production. Yes, we are living in the Thousand-Year Reign of Christ. To summarize an earlier statement, Christianity has filled the earth powerfully since the first century, humanity is notably more blessed with long lives, prosperity, and greater peace in these days rather than at any other time in history. "In the areas where Christianity emerged two thousand years ago, people were much more barbaric than they are today. Conflict was everywhere. Human sacrifice, including that of children, was a common occurrence even in the technologically sophisticated societies, such as that of ancient Carthage."[37] "In Rome, arena sports were competitions to the death, and the spilling of blood was a commonplace. The probability that a modern person, in a functional democratic country, will now kill or be killed is infinitesimally low compared to what it was in previous societies (and still is, in the unorganized and anarchic parts of the world."[38] "People with those aggressive tendencies still exist. At least now they know that such behavior is sub-optimal, and either try to control it or encounter major social obstacles if they don't."[39] Yes, Christ's reign began and is continuing, and we are living in it today. May the Lord be praised!

How Can You Say That the Kingdom Is Growing Today?

That is a plausible statement to make if you are honest with the results Christianity has made throughout history since the first century. The irrefutable results of Christ's work on the cross, God's continuing Providence in the earth, and the work of His Church since the first century have resulted in incremental trends upward with regard to mankind living longer and more justly toward

---

[37] Salisbury, J.E. (1997). Perpetua's Passion: The death and memory of a young Roman woman. New York: Routledge as quoted in Jordan Peterson's 12 Rules For Life, An Antidote to Chaos, p. 58.

[38] Pinker, S. (2011). The Better Angels of Our Nature: Why violence has declined. New York: Viking Books as quoted in Jordan Peterson's 12 Rules For Life, An Antidote to Chaos, p. 58.

[39] Peterson, Jordan, 12 Rules For Life, An Antidote to Chaos, p. 58.

one another, as well as more prosperously, and with more liberty and abundant life than ever before in history. Yes, there have been cultural zeniths in which the Law of God prevailed in the culture, such as in the Carolingian Empire, the Catholic Hapsburg Empire, 16th Century Geneva, etc.; however, there have been the troughs of pagan cultural victories, such as the move to reclaim secularism, subdue Christianity, and in some cases restore a neo-paganism associated with Julian the Apostate in Ancient Rome, the human sacrificing Myans, the taking of Constantinople by the Ottoman Turks, Hitler's Germany, and Stalin's U.S.S.R. Yet, even after World Wars I and II, the trend has been that multitudes more of humanity come to know Christ and learn of His ways in the Church. They leaven the culture and have made it more peaceful than the preceding generations. The Lord Jesus has been preached in every nation and nearly to all of mankind on the face of the earth. Although there are still wars here and there due to the lust of men's hearts, as St. James has written,[40] the world has not experienced the devastating wars of the early nineteenth and twentieth centuries, nor do we see major advances of one powerful nation to destroy another nation and wipe out its Christian heritage as has been seen in the past. This is the result of God's grace in Christ. This is the Kingdom of God leavening the earth until the entire earth is full of the Word and glory of God. Christian and peace-loving unbelieving nations now understand what nuclear destruction, fascist regimes, lawless societies and cultures of death can cause and want no part of it, or at least want less of it than in years before. The same now see that wide-spread and cultural obedience to God's Law is the remedy for these ills. World leaders, educators, bishops, those in business and professional life, and citizens in all lands are being touched by God's grace in Christ to pray in faith, "Thy Kingdom come, Thy will be done ON EARTH AS IT IS IN HEAVEN." As a result, the Church is witnessing massive numbers of Christian conversions at present in China, Africa, and Iran.

Isaiah prophesied about blessings that would progressively come in the earth as the inaugurated New Heavens and New Earth continued to be realized.[41] It is

---

[40] James 4:1-6.

[41] Isa 65-66.

written in Scripture that the deserts will bloom like a rose and will continue to do so to the extent that Christ's Church obeys the Lord and continues to disciple the nations, and to the extent that those who hear the commandments of the Lord obey them. The late R. J. Rushdoony, a noted theologian in the twentieth century, stated in his <u>First the Blade</u> article, that we pray for the Kingdom of God to come daily, and we expect incremental results, but not necessarily quick or immediate results in the growth of God's Kingdom. He goes on to tell us:

> "…when we plant grain, we must cultivate it, often water it, tend to the field, and, only after much labor, reap a harvest. To expect otherwise is presumptuous, stupidity and foolishness, whether in farming or in the work of the Kingdom. In fact, our Lord describes quick growth as false (Matt 13:5-6, 20-21). The parables about the growth of the Kingdom of God have as their purpose to make us diligent and patient (James 5:7-11). Is it any wonder that evil churchmen have neglected Mark 4:28? Our Lord is very clear: the pattern of the Kingdom of God is like that of the earth which bringeth forth fruit of itself. There is an order and a progression from the seed, to the first green shoot to emerge, to the cultivated growth, and finally the harvest. Both time and work are essential."[42]

How Can You Say Satan is Bound Now?

Satan has not only been defeated by our Lord's work on the cross, in which Jesus disarmed the demonic principalities and powers and made a public spectacle of them, but our Lord Jesus also bound Him after His coming with His Kingdom in great power in A.D. 70.[43] The devil's binding and being held in

---

[42] R.J.Rushdoony, First the Blade, Chalcedon. https://chalcedon.edu/resources/articles/first-the-blade

[43] John 12:31; 16:11; and Rev 12:4,7-12; 20:1-3. John sees Satan dispatching a third of the demons to destroy the Christ Child, and during His ministry, Christ Jesus sees the devil cast out of the heavens with a third of the angels and thrown to earth. In the Revelation, John sees the devil and

the abyss, or bottomless pit, means that he has been rendered impotent as to deceiving the nations regarding the truth that Jesus is Christ is Lord and King of the Kingdom of God. Catholic exorcist, Fr. Carlos Martins, says it well when he says that God has Satan on a leash. Satan can do nothing in this period of history, during the reign of Christ, without God's sovereign permission. He also states that "one confession is worth a thousand exorcisms." This means that during Christ's reign, though we can see active evil, our obedience to God's Law and our participation in the Mass and the Sacraments severely reduces Satan's powers to operate. Obedience to Scripture and refusal to enter into relationship with Satan in any way (e.g., participation in occult activities) is sufficiently the normal course of Providence since Christ's Death and Resurrection, keeping Satan's powers bound. And we who believe in Christ's work can pray the binding prayers of the Church in Jesus' Name and be assured of the power of those prayers to succeed when coupled with lives of obedience.[44] This is why this period in history is sometimes called the "Feast of Ingathering," symbolic of all nations of the world coming to Zion to hear and obey the Word of the Lord and pay obeisance to Jesus Christ as Lord and King. As a result of the devil's binding, God now commands men everywhere to repent and to believe the Gospel of the Kingdom of God. Jesus Christ has been building His Church and the gates of hell do not prevail against the Church. Today, in the reign of Christ, we see that the only thing stopping the advance of the Kingdom is not the power of Satan, but the unbelief and disobedience of mankind who either hear the truth and do not obey it, or who are ignorant of the truths of the Christian faith. During these days, we are commanded to love God and love our neighbors, obeying everything Christ commanded. In our doing that, God brings all things under His Son's feet; that is, God subdues all wickedness under Christ in time. A defeated and bound Satan tells lies and lay a shroud of lies over the nations, tempting them to sin, blinding them to righteousness and justice, and pressing a secularization of culture leading to societal sin, corruption and the ultimate judgment of collapse.

---

his angels cast to the earth to incite the Great Tribulation three and one half years before the Lord Jesus would bind them and place them in the abyss during Christ's Thousand-Year Reign.

[44] An excellent book on binding prayers is <u>Deliverance Prayers</u>, For Use by the Laity, by Fr. Chad Ripperger, PhD.

For the individual, this is the path to hell. To avoid this trajectory, Christians must remain vigilant and knowledgeable of Satan's binding by Christ nearly two thousand years ago so as not to become distracted by the world, its lusts and lies, and its vices. The Church must, therefore, arise, and press the crown rights of Christ's Kingdom into every realm of life by evangelizing mankind. This leads to times of refreshing from the Lord and great blessings of righteousness, peace, and joy associated with the Kingdom of God's presence now in these days.

What about the Antichrist?

St. John is the only one in Sacred Scripture who speaks of the Antichrist and the spirit of antichrist in his first and second epistles. Although he says that there were many antichrists in the world at that time, John specifically states that in *his day*, which was the last hour prior to the Great Tribulation, the Antichrist was coming. This Antichrist was prophesied by Daniel as one of the Roman rulers, or emperors. Many theologians and historians have concluded that this Antichrist was Caesar Nero, the man of sin (lawlessness), the son of perdition,[45] who became a manifest persecutor of the Church about the time Jerusalem's priesthood ceased praying for and sacrificing animals daily to the Roman emperor. This ceasing of temple sacrifices on behalf of the emperor of Rome is what historians believe began Rome's war against the Jews leading eventually within three-and one-half years to the fall of Jerusalem.

Nero's wickedness knew no bounds. He allegedly started the great fire of Rome and then falsely blamed the Christians for the crime. He was a violent and perverted homosexual who murdered his wife and his tutor, Seneca. He would dress as a wild animal and sexually molest prisoners. He sought to change the name of Rome to Neropolis. He covered those convicted of believing in Christ Jesus with pitch and burned them to light his garden parties. Nero also delighted in torturing Christians in the Colosseum games. He held Christ in contempt

---

[45] 2 Thess 2:2-4.

and spoke pompous words against the Lord and His Christ during the time of great trouble for Israel and the Church.[46]

Not only theological but also historical study of this time in history helps us to get ourselves into the mind of the Apostle John who wrote the Revelation of Jesus Christ for the churches and into the minds of the readers and hearers of that message. It is absolutely impossible to come to correct conclusions about the Antichrist without examining religious and historical studies of these first century events. Not only is the Book of Revelation our anchor of truth on this but also Josephus' work, The Wars of the Jews, helps us to interpret the Revelation correctly and relevantly *in that time*. For example, we see two beasts in Rev 13: the Beast arising from the sea, which Philip Schaff defines as the Roman Empire;[47] and the beast arising from the land, which David Chilton, in his Days of Vengeance, defines as the false prophet of apostate Jerusalem that arises from the *Promised Land*.[48] The image of the Beast from the Sea was a man, an emperor, yet he represents the wicked line of emperors that succeeded him after his suicidal death.[49] This author is in agreement with a significant number of historians and theologians who are convinced that the man whose number was 666 correlated with Caesar Nero's name, when spelled and read in Ancient Hebrew.[50]

The Antichrist Caesar Nero eventually committed suicide in A.D. 68, sending the Roman Empire into political turmoil and making the Great Tribulation even more intense. This great distress would last an additional two years until A.D. 70. At Christ's Parousia, the Antichrist, Nero, was cast into the Lake of Fire and will not rise again.

---

[46] Dan 12:1; Matt 24:21. Also see Schaff's summary on Nero in Table 4..

[47] Rev 13:1-10 interpreted in Schaff's, History of Christianity, Vol. I, Apostolic Christianity, pp. 852-853.

[48] Rev 13:11-14 interpreted in Chilton's, Days of Vengeance, pp. 335-344.

[49] Rev 13:12-18.

[50] Each Ancient Hebrew letter had an assigned numerical value. When all of the consonants in Caesar Nero's name were summed (spelled and read as NeRoN KeSaR), the title and name total 666. See Gentry's, The Beast of the Revelation.

It should be noted that since that time there have been and will be those who are and who succumb to false prophets. There will be those who give themselves over to the spirit of Antichrist. These, however, are not the same as *the Antichrist* of the first century Great Tribulation, Caesar Nero, the image of the Beast, and the one whose number was 666. That is past. We have no biblical evidence to believe that when the devil is loosed from his binding at the end of Christ's Thousand-Year Reign, there would be another Beast, or image of the Beast, or another whose number is 666. The last days are behind us, and our days of victory are ahead; therefore, we can sing the victory Song of Moses as did the children of Israel and the overcomers of the Great Tribulation who held firm their testimony of Christ to overcome Satan, the world, and the Antichrist of the first century.[51]

Why Did You Write This Book?

This book draws from my 42 years of studying the Kingdom of God, both for seminary and for my own personal interest, and its definitive and progressive comings throughout redemptive history. It also summarizes my recommendations for how one should live and resolve the frustrations of the seeming contradictions between God's Kingdom having come and its continuing to come in the earth until the end. Intrigued by the recency of dispensational doctrine, I was interested in knowing the non-fantastical truths about last things and what was the sense of the prophets', Jesus', and the Church's words about the King and His Kingdom. This interest was especially fueled by so many preachers, teachers, and friends around me who were well convinced that Jesus was returning to "rapture the church" in 1988, the same year I had planned my wedding. Contrary to my Christian friend's belief in Jesus' immanent return that year, I married my wife, Jesus didn't return, the world didn't end, and neither were we transported to heaven in escape of a Great Tribulation. While on our honeymoon in Gatlinburg, Tennessee, my wife and I spent one evening in a local church where the late Pastor David Chilton (1951–1997) was guest speaker. Dr. Chilton had just published

---

[51] Ex 15:1-21; also c.f., Deut 32:1-43; Rev 15:1-4.

three amazingly substantive books on eschatology: Paradise Restored (1985), Days of Vengeance (1987), and The Great Tribulation (1987), all of which are still available. He spoke authoritatively about the ancient Church's saints, such as Athanasius and Irenaeus, and how they believed wholeheartedly that Jesus Christ was the reigning King and that His reign would bring tangible blessings to the Church and the entire earth. Chilton taught that the Kingdom was expanding now in these days and that the Great Tribulation happened to the early church in the first century. I particularly loved how he exhorted fathers to teach these truths to their children as did the saints of old to build godly heritages within the Church, full of hope for the future victory of Christ's Kingdom on earth. I am documenting findings that I believe will be helpful in rooting and grounding Christians in where they stand in redemptive history today as priests and kings unto God in His growing Kingdom. These truths affect how we, our children, and our grandchildren live in Christ.

I have included some commentary on the Revelation of Jesus Christ to show the relevance and connection of the Last Days to the first century Jews, Jerusalem, and its temple. Given that the Kingdom of God has come in power and is still coming progressively as God brings heaven to earth, I have also added my synopsis of the wisdom gained from the Book of Ecclesiastes to provide help and resolve when considering the vexing observations seen in a sinful world while it is being cleaned and redeemed over time by Christ's building His Church, expanding His Kingdom, and bidding all nations to come and hear the Word of the Lord.

Christ's Kingdom, His Church, is imperialistic. Jesus will neither fail nor be discouraged until His laws fill the earth.[52] Through the Gospel of the Kingdom, the Church declares to the world a loving message of, as one of the late Dr. Gary North's books with the same title described it, "unconditional surrender." The alternative to believing and obeying this loving message of the King is that of being crushed to powder.[53] Since the first century, Christianity has filled the earth so that there seems to be no nation that in some way does not know something of Christ Jesus. This faith in a reigning King Jesus who blesses the righteous and

---

[52] Is 42:4.

[53] Matt 21:34.

gives grace to subdue the earth to Christendom is what led the Roman bishops to send St. Patrick to England and Ireland, the Portuguese to send missionaries to Asia, and the Dutch to send priests and pastors to India and Africa. Those who oppose Christ, such as the global secularists, are just temporary impediments that will be moved out of the way, either through repentance and the relinquishing of their weapons, or by their being crushed to powder, trampled by mankind, and ultimately being forgotten in history. May we get excited about praying and believing that God's Kingdom come while we're building families, estates, cities and nations, and generations of peoples to the glory of God as He brings heaven to earth under the Lordship of the Messiah King, Jesus.

TABLE 1: THE MYSTERY OF THE KINGDOM OF GOD UNFOLDING TO REVEAL THE NUMBERED DAYS OF ISRAEL

Table 1 sets the stage for showing us the origin and reason for the term "last days." The two chronological timelines in this table begin with man's cultural mandate; then progresses to his redemption from sin through a Messiah to come; and then establishes the covenantal family line of prophets, priests, and kings through Jacob, whose name would be changed to Israel. You will note the unfolding nature of the Kingdom of God through Israel, a nation of priests and kings, which was but a type and shadow—a forerunner nation and kingdom—of a new and better Kingdom to come in Christ Jesus. You will see in "*Chronological Timeline 2*," for the first time in Sacred Scripture the term "last days," which is applied to the days of Old Testament Israel and its civil, moral, and redemptive laws, which include her liturgical worship of God, whose proper name is Yahweh. *Chronological Timeline 2* begins with Jacob speaking to His sons, known as the twelve tribes of Israel, in Genesis 49:1-2, "Gather together, that I may tell you what shall befall you in the *last days*."[54] Jacob proceeds to tell each tribe how they fit into God's Providential plan leading to Messiah Prince, Jesus. In both *Chronological Timelines 1 and 2*, the Old Covenant (also known as the First Covenant) is established and the New Covenant is promised.

Tables 2-4 will follow the progress of Old Covenant Israel and its predicted demise, while revealing more clearly God's plan to save out of the Old Covenant nation of Israel a new, better, born-again nation of priests and kings based on a new and better covenant. This is the New Jerusalem: the New Heavens and

---

[54] This is an example of the application of the hermeneutical tool called, "analogy of Scripture," in which one allows clear and easy to understand passages of Scripture to assist in interpreting more difficult passages of Scripture. In this example, we let the term "last days," (as found in the Genesis passage) support our conclusion that the last days in New Testament Scripture refer to the last days of Old Covenant Israel.

Earth that would come in Yahweh incarnate, Jesus the Christ—the time in which we now live.

God Gave You a Cultural Mandate to Fulfill

From our vantage point in redemptive history we know from Scripture that Jesus Christ, the Word of God, the Second Person of the Trinity, was the Lamb of God slain, or sacrificed, for the sins of mankind from the foundation of the world, in other words, the universe's beginning.[55] God foreknew the sin of Adam and the derivative original and actual sin of mankind prior to His creating Adam. And in eternity past,[56] God redeemed mankind through the promised Christ, the Eternal Word of the Father, from his sin. It is also clear that God had intended to create for Himself a holy people, set apart and beloved, who would be His special nation, His exclusive and chosen inheritance of prophets, priests, and kings among the nations beginning with Adam, the first man. Adam was created to be a vicegerent in the earth representing God, His rule, His light, His law, and His love. God told Adam to be fruitful, multiply and replenish the earth, work and subdue it, and have dominion.[57]

---

[55] Rev 13:8; John 17:24.

[56] A theologically speculative term to describe the time frame prior to time beginning with the creation of the heavens and the earth.

[57] Gen 1:28.

Table 1. The Mystery of the Kingdom of God Unfolding to Reveal the Numbered Days of Israel

Unfolding Covenant of Grace / Unfolding nature of the Kingdom of God and His Christ in types and shadows

Chronological Timeline 1

Cultural Mandate
Be fruitful, multiply, subdue the earth, have dominion, Gen 1:28.

Protoevangelium
The Child shall crush the Serpent's head, Gen 3:15.

3090 B.C. Covenant with Noah
Affirmed Cultural Mandate, Gen 9:1.

1910 B.C. Covenant of Abraham
Promise to make him a father of many nations; people as the sea sand. God will be his shield, and his reward will be great, Gen 15 and 17.

1500 B.C. God's Grace Begets the First Covenant
At Sinai with Moses, later Jerusalem, the City of the Great King, to be referred to as "Old." I will be your God and you will be My people and enlarge your borders, Lev 26:12, Exod 34:24.

This First Covenant of Grace became the Whole Heaven & Earth to the Jew
Jerusalem, the City of the Great King, the footstool of God, the earth
• Temple: Dwelling place of Yahweh
• The Promised Land
• Redemptive system
• Sacrifices / blood atonement
• Levitical priesthood
• Temple furniture: table of shewbread, lampstand, the Ark of Covenant, altar of incense, the Holiest Place for the Jews to know the will of God

The Sum of the Commands of the First Covenant: Deut 10:12 "And now, Israel, what does the Lord your God require of you, but to fear the Lord your God, to walk in all his ways, to serve the Lord your God with all your heart and with all your soul, 13 and to keep the commandments and statutes of the Lord, which I command you this day for your good? 14 Behold, to the Lord your God belong heaven and the heaven of heavens, the earth with all that is in it; 15 yet the Lord set his heart in love upon your fathers and chose their descendants after them, you above all peoples, as at this day."

The True Jew is One Whose Heart is Circumcised: Rom 2: 28 For he is not a real Jew who is one outwardly, nor is true circumcision something external and physical. 29 He is a Jew who is one inwardly, and real circumcision is a matter of the heart, spiritual and not literal. His praise is not from men but from God.

In 586 B.C. Jerusalem taken captive to Babylon due to her continued unrepentant sin, 2 Kgs, Jer, Lam.

Chronological Timeline 2

1460 B.C. First Mention of a Last Days For Old Testament Israel & Jerusalem
In Israel's *latter*/last days, a King will come from Judah. There was a beginning, and there would be an end, Deut 4, Gen 49:8-12.

1012 B.C. A Coming Eternal King & Kingdom
King David of Judah's offspring would succeed as King, and this King would build a house for God's name and a Kingdom that would last forever, 2 Sam 7:12.

Coming Son of David
The King would suffer and reign w/a New Covenant w/justice and His Law out of Jerusalem/Zion & this Kingdom will fill the earth, Isa 2, 42, 53; Jer.31:31; Ps(s) 2, 110.

A New Covenant & New Heavens and New Earth
The Old Testament prophets affirmed the previous covenantal promises in terms of a New Covenant. I will be your God and you will be My people I will cast out the nations and enlarge your borders, Lev 26:12. The Law of God would be written on the heart of His people to know it and do it, Jer 31:31-34.

Features of the New Heavens and New Earth
• Justice, righteousness, peace
• Rejoicing, walking in God's light/Law
• Spirit of God writing the Law of God on the heart to know and do God's will
• Deserts blooming like a rose over time
• All nations worshipping Christ the King
• Weapons of war turned to implements of production, and war is learned no more
• Every man and his descendants blessed
• Zion, the New Jerusalem is the dwelling place of God
• Whole world is holy
Isa 65:17; Ps(s) 1, Mic. 4, Ezek 43-48.

The Kingdom of Israel, a Type of the Kingdom of God, Has a Set Number of Days
The Israelites knew first from Moses and then from the prophets that the Christ would come in the latter, or last days of the Kingdom of Israel, Jerusalem. The term "*latter*," or "*last days*," develops as history progresses. *Table 2* provides significant detail regarding the last days within the context of Daniel's 70 Weeks Prophecy recorded in Dan 9:20-27.

This was man's cultural mandate from God: Walk with God in obedience; bear a godly seed (offspring) to fill the earth; subdue the resources of the earth to God's glory and to man's enjoyment; continue to build, explore, subdue, and work the earth to the glory of God to the end of time.[58] This belief motivated Christian explorers and missionaries to bring the Gospel of the Kingdom of God and this mandate to nations across the earth. Mankind, through the watchful Providence and blessing of his faithful God, was to bring God's kingdom to earth and expand it as he himself spread across the face of the earth. Man was to build and steward the creation and glorify God in works of faith, hope, and love in every realm of life. These realms of life included purifying and setting apart his own life and making God-glorifying contributions to the world through his family, the State, education, business, and other institutions.

Adam was to be affirmed in eternal life through this obedience; however, through sin, through yielding to Satan's temptation, Adam forfeited his kingdom role of vicegerent and his estate of abundant and eternal life in exchange for that estate of death. This was the result of his eating of the Tree of Knowledge of Good and Evil versus partaking of the Tree of Life as God had commanded him. He instead acted on the Tempter's lie. It is at this time that one saw an affront, a confrontation, a battle between God's Kingdom and the purpose of Satan, a real, spiritual, and personal adversary. Satan lives to kill, steal, and destroy God's creation and to deceive mankind with promises that appeal to man's lust of the flesh, lust of the eyes, and pride of life. Through man's free will, he chose the lies of Satan resulting in his fall from God's grace and his being cut off from God without hope in the world. Adam was excommunicated from the Garden as part of the consequences he, his wife, and his progeny would bear for his unethical decision to reject loyalty to his faithful God and the blessings of His Kingdom. He forfeited the paradise of Eden. Satan then possessed a realm over which he could exercise a deceptive dominion, namely mankind itself and the creation over which *man* was to rule. It would seem that Satan had won. However, even though Adam, his wife, and his future children had lost the paradisical Kingdom

---

[58] C.f., A morning prayer in the Catholic Breviary, May 30, 2023, lbreviary.com: "You instructed man to labor and to exercise dominion over the earth, - may our work honor you and sanctify our brothers and sisters. Hear us, O Lord, for the glory of your name."

of God on earth, God Himself would now redeem mankind through a promise of a Second Adam namely the Christ to come. The man would now have to rely on God's unmerited favor, His grace, to be redeemed and to see the redemption of his wife and his future children. Only through the redeeming work of God, an act referred to as the Protoevangelium, could mankind be restored to his position of being a God-fearing and God-glorifying vicegerent of God Himself and be restored to fulfilling the cultural mandate in righteousness, peace, and joy to work to establish heaven on earth.

The Hope of the Gospel of Christ Was Established by God in the Garden: the Protoevangelium

It was gracious of God, who is rich in mercy, to permit Adam to live after His sin. God would bring both consequences for the sin and a promise of redemption to Adam. After all, the Christ who would be promised to Adam, the Seed of the woman, was preordained as slain, as it is written, from the foundations of the world. Moses wrote in Gen 3:15, that which God said to the serpent, Satan, after he had deceived the man, tempted him, and caused him to stumble, "And I will put enmity between you and the woman, and between your seed and her Seed; He shall bruise your head, and you shall bruise His heel."

This was the Gospel message to Adam that pointed him to Jesus Christ, the Seed who would come from the Virgin Mary. This passage is called the Protoevangelium because it is God's evangelistic, message of "good news" to Adam of salvation through Christ Jesus 4000 years prior to Christ's coming to earth. From the moment that message was delivered by God, the true religion of the one true God, Yahweh, would be based upon belief in the Seed to come. In other words, faith in the Seed, who would later be referred to as the Christ, or Messiah, was the only way mankind could gain favor with God and receive His blessings. Belief in the Seed to come enabled Adam, his wife, and his children after him, through his son Seth, to be restored to the capability to fulfill the cultural mandate. Christianity, therefore, began in the Garden by promise, and was always the one, true religion of Yahweh God. This hope of the Christ to come was salvific to the true Jews—those who were indeed circumcised in heart and not just in the flesh.[59] The Seed of Adam's wife, Eve, namely Jesus to come, would crush the head of the seed of the Adversary, the same one who tempted Adam to his sin and brought forth his downfall. From that time forward, all of creation would await the revealing of the sons of God so that all of nature itself also would be free from the bondage of sin. Since the Protoevangelium, mankind and nature would await a second Adam, Jesus, the Christ, and Messiah King to come, born of a Virgin, referred to by the Church as the Second Eve. While waiting, Adam and his children after him would establish a covenant family line from whom would come Noah, Abraham, Isaac, and Jacob, whose twelve children would become the holy covenantal nation of Israel who would be called to walk in holiness before Yahweh. This nation, which would have *a set number of days* associated with its existence, would be a type and shadow of Christ's Kingdom to come. Finally, it should be noted that all of God's chosen people since Adam believed in a Christ to come, and all of those living during and after Christ believed in the Christ who had come. Therefore, all of God's chosen people since the beginning can rightly be called Christian.

God Confirmed with Noah the Cultural Mandate to Build

Adam and Eve bore a son named Seth, a new son who "replaces" Abel who was murdered by Cain, who obeyed God and carried on the family lineage and its promise of a Seed that would crush the seed of the serpent. When Adam and Eve's son, Cain, murdered their righteous son Abel, we witnessed the continuing confrontation between the growing Kingdom of God on earth through covenant families and the persistent rebellion of covenant breakers inspired by Satan, the

---

[59] Rom 2:28. The term "Jew" as St. Paul has written, transcends the name of a people simply born of the Tribe of Judah. The Jew is now seen in the New Testament as a covenantal term applied to one who has been given a new heart by the Spirit of God through the new birth (being born again or having partook of a spiritual conversion of heart by God's Spirit). We conclude that all who believed in a Christ to come (Jesus), as well as those who have believed on Christ since His resurrection are all "true Jews," or Christians. Hence "Christianity" has always been the true religion of the one true God, whose name is "Yahweh." The name of Jesus means "Yahweh Saves."

same serpent of old, whose delight is in the destruction of families who fear and love God and keep His commandments.[60] During these days, nearly 4000 years before Christ's birth, due to the wickedness of men growing evil beyond reparation, God executed judgment upon mankind and flooded the earth destroying all creation except for a descendant of Seth, namely Noah, and his family of eight.[61] After the Flood had ended and Noah and his family were saved on dry land, God made a covenant with Noah, gave him specific laws, the promise of seasons, and the assurance via the rainbow that the earth would never be thoroughly flooded again. God affirmed His original Cultural Mandate to Noah and his descendants to be fruitful and multiply, bring forth abundantly upon the earth, and subdue it. God even put the fear of Noah and his sons upon all the creatures. The Kingdom of God and man's vicegerency thus continued forward, the temptations and gates of hell not stopping them. Man's faith remained in God's promise of the Messiah to come, the Seed of the woman. Again, by God's grace, the Kingdom of God from this covenant family led by a believing head of household, Noah, ensured the continuing growth, knowledge, and influence of the Kingdom of God, which would continue to bring salvation, strength, and the power of the promised Christ to all with whom the covenant people would interface.

God Confirmed with Abraham That His Heritage Would Fill the Earth and Be Blessed

As the Kingdom of God grew, there were those who did not want to go forth and replenish the entire earth and subdue it. They thought of a "better plan" to assemble in one place to avoid being scattered over the earth. They built a tower to their own glory to heaven. God saw their disobedient, cowardly, self-glorifying, and faithless actions and judged them by confusing their languages. The place was called "Babel" for that was where man's tribal languages were confused and relegated to babbling, non-discernable communications causing confusion and

---

[60] Rev 12:9; 20:2. Satan, the serpent of old, the devil, and the adversary all are synonymous for the same being.

[61] Gen 5-9.

the end of the centralization plot. This was a proof that when the kingdoms of men under the reign of sin and death, inspired by Satan, seek to plot against God and His Christ, God laughs in heaven for the nations even when all conspiring together, are as nothing before the Living God.[62]

Soon after those days, God reached out to a man named Abram, a righteous descendent of Noah's son Shem (from where we get the term "Semite"), and Shem's descendent Eber (where we get the ethnic name, "Hebrew"). God chose Abram (a name meaning "high father") to follow Him and continue the building of His Kingdom. God made a covenant with Abram giving him the name, "Abraham" meaning "father of many nations."[63] God affirmed that he would be great in all of the earth, thus affirming the Covenant of Grace in the Garden and the cultural mandate to subdue the earth to Yahweh's glory. Abram is recorded in Scripture as having met Melchizedek, the King of Salem and the Priest of God Most High, Yahweh.[64] Melchizedek, a type and shadow of the promised Seed to come, Jesus Christ, the Great High Priest,[65] blessed Abram, for which Abram promised to give a tenth to God of everything of his from that time onward. *Chronological Timeline 1* shows that Abraham and his wife, both of whom were significantly beyond childbearing age, would bear a son, from whom the promise the Kingdom of God would continue and grow with a vast number of covenant children numbered as many as the sand of the seashore. This Abrahamic Covenant was a blessing and an affirmation of the continuity of God's Cultural Mandate and a faith in the Christ to come.

God's blessing of this deeper cut in the Covenant of Grace continued from Abraham to his son Isaac, and then passed to Isaac's son Jacob, whose name was changed to Israel, who would beget twelve sons who would lead the twelve tribes of Israel (also known as the children of Israel, the covenant people, the Old Testament church, or the assembly in the wilderness). Providentially, Esau, the firstborn son of Isaac, to whom the blessing would normally have passed,

---

[62] Ps(s) 2.

[63] Gen 12, 15, 17.

[64] Gen 14:17-23.

[65] Heb 7.

sinned and sold the covenantal blessing of his birthright to his brother Jacob for a pot of stew.[66]

As to Esau, his seed throughout redemptive history brought continual confrontation and grief to the children of Israel. Esau's line included the Idumeans, from whom Herod the Great came. He sought to kill the Christ after His birth by putting to death all the male children who were in Bethlehem and in all its districts, from two years old and under, according to the timeline which he had determined from the Magi of Persia.[67] This act of Herod clearly depicted the continuing attempt of Satan to stop the advance of the Kingdom of God and to continue the deception of his dominion over the world.

The Kingdom of God grows in the earth when the covenant people of God, His Church, embrace the faith of Abraham, Isaac, and Jacob, who believed in God and His promised Christ, and who worshiped, obeyed, and loved Him as St. Paul wrote, "Therefore know that only those who are of faith are the sons of Abraham. And the Scripture, foreseeing that God would justify the Gentiles by faith, preached the Gospel to Abraham beforehand, saying, 'In you all the nations shall be blessed.' So then those who are of faith are blessed with believing Abraham."[68]

God's "First Covenant" with Israel Was Their Entire Heavens and Earth

We come to a definitive point in redemptive history when God comes with His armies of angels upon Mount Sinai to make a covenant with the children of Israel through their prophet and mediator, a descendant of Abraham, Moses. This, of course, happened after the exodus from Egypt, which occurred sometime around 1500-1440 B.C. This meeting between God and His people

---

[66] Gen 25:33; Heb 12:16.

[67] Matt 2:16-18.

[68] Gal 3:7-9.

established the relational and covenantal truth that God would be their God, and that they would be His special people, His own inheritance of all peoples among the nations. God also declared that the children of Israel were a kingdom, as God had said in the past, "Now therefore, if you obey My voice and keep My covenant, you shall be My treasured possession out of all the peoples. Indeed, the whole earth is Mine, but you shall be for Me a priestly kingdom and a holy nation."[69] God affirms the cultural mandate for His people to rule over the creation to God's glory. His people were to have faith in the Christ to come (the Protoevangelium). God clearly told this assembly in the wilderness of Sinai that He would raise up from among his covenant people a Prophet who would speak Yahweh God's words. Furthermore, the children of Israel were going to be held accountable for their obedience to this Prophet's voice, which would be the voice of the Christ to come.[70] These words again affirm that the number of Old Covenant Israel's days were numbered, and there would be a last days of this first covenant arrangement. This first covenant between Yahweh God and the children of Israel was ratified by the sacrificial blood of bulls and goats, a ratification that was a type and shadow of the future New Covenant between God and His people. This New Covenant would be between God and His chosen people from both the Jewish and Gentile nations, who would be made into one people together in Christ Jesus. This New Covenant would be ratified, not by the blood of animals, but by the Blood of the Lamb of God, Jesus Christ. All who would believe in and obey Jesus Christ, as foretold and typified via the elements of the first covenant, would be saved and possess eternal life. As the children of Israel, led by Joshua and Caleb entered the Promised Land, their settled tribes and their liturgical focal point of Jerusalem and its temple where God's presence would dwell would represent a temporal and shakable Kingdom, which would stand as a type and shadow of the Kingdom of God in heaven. Eventually, the temporal nation of Israel, its Jerusalem, and its temple would be shaken to the ground to give way to the New Jerusalem and the New Heavens and New Earth. When

---

[69] Exod 19:5-6.

[70] Deut 18:15-16.

the foundational construction of the new was complete, the scaffolding of the old would drop to the ground, never to be erected again.[71]

The Kingdom of Israel would also consist of the most important touch point between God and man, the Jerusalem temple, which housed the Ark of the Covenant, the resting place of God's presence within the temple's Holy of Holies (the innermost sanctuary). This first temple was built by King Solomon, son of King David, around 950 B.C.[72] The Ark of the Covenant also housed the tablets of the Ten Commandments. This first covenant established the holy furniture and where its components would be placed within the temple, including the table of shewbread, the lampstand, and the golden altar of incense.

God's law, His direct revelation of His will to His people was given through Moses as part of the first covenant. The law consisted of the ceremonial, or redemptive laws, concerning sacrifices, holy liturgical practices, and blood atonement, which made a way of redemption from sin for the people. There were also juridical or civil laws pertaining to the civil affairs of the children of Israel that would pass away with the theocratic nation. Finally, there were the ceremonial and moral laws. The ceremonial laws were fulfilled and continue to be fulfilled in Christ Jesus; however, the moral laws, the Commandments of God pertaining to discerning right, wrong, and the blessings and punishments associated with doing good or evil, are still in force and were affirmed as being so by Jesus Christ.[73] Obedience to the full set of these laws as the ethical component of the first covenant were considered to be the tools of dominion for the covenant people to fulfill the cultural mandate. Israel, the nation of kings and priests, would be blessed if she feared Yahweh and obeyed Him; loved Him with all of her heart, soul, and mind; and loved her neighbor as herself. Curses were the sanction for disobedience.

God spoke through Moses:

---

[71] Heb 12:22-24.

[72] 1 Kings 5-8.

[73] Matt 5:17-20.

Now it shall come to pass, if you diligently obey the voice of the Lord your God, to observe carefully all His commandments which I command you today, that the Lord your God will set you high above all nations of the earth. And all these blessings shall come upon you and overtake you, because you obey the voice of the Lord your God: "Blessed shall you be in the city, and blessed shall you be in the country. Blessed shall be the fruit of your body, the produce of your ground and the increase of your herds, the increase of your cattle and the offspring of your flocks. Blessed shall be your basket and your kneading bowl. Blessed shall you be when you come in, and blessed shall you be when you go out. The Lord will cause your enemies who rise against you to be defeated before your face; they shall come out against you one way and flee before you seven ways. The Lord will command the blessing on you in your storehouses and in all to which you set your hand, and He will bless you in the land which the Lord your God is giving you. The Lord will establish you as a holy people to Himself, just as He has sworn to you, if you keep the commandments of the Lord your God and walk in His ways. Then all peoples of the earth shall see that you are called by the name of the Lord, and they shall be afraid of you. And the Lord will grant you plenty of goods, in the fruit of your body, in the increase of your livestock, and in the produce of your ground, in the land of which the Lord swore to your fathers to give you. The Lord will open to you His good treasure, the heavens, to give the rain to your land in its season, and to bless all the work of your hand. You shall lend to many nations, but you shall not borrow. And the Lord will make you the head and not the tail; you shall be above only, and not be beneath, if you heed the commandments of the Lord your God, which I command you today, and are careful to observe them. So you shall not turn aside from any of the words which I command you this day, to the right or the left, to go after other gods to serve them."[74]

It is interesting to note that there are 14 verses in Deut 28 that declare these wonderful blessings for obedience; however, there are 54 verses of curses that follow verse 14 that would come upon the people of Israel should they disobey. And they did. And the curses followed.

This first covenant between God and the children of Israel at Sinai gave them not only the revealed will of God, a Promised Land, a temple and the promise of blessings for obedient behavior, but it also gave the nation a Levitical priesthood, which was a temporary liturgical mediatorship with Aaron, the high priest, and his descendants. It is critical to note here that this moral, redemptive, liturgical, and priestly relationship between God and His people was considered by the Jewish people to be the entire and comprehensive "heaven on earth." The first covenant, the Promised Land, the tabernacle of meeting, and Yahweh's laws were the entire world to the children of Israel. This covenant between God and His people based on faith in the Seed, the Prophet and High Priest to come, represented the first principles, or the substantive elements of the first heaven and earth, the reality of which was entrenched deep into the hearts of God's people.

Understanding this covenantal relationship between Yahweh God and His people, the children of Israel, or the Jews, as they would be referred to after the Exile around 537 B.C., will be critical in understanding how the first century Christians from among the Jews and Gentiles would perceive the prophecies of a New Heaven and New Earth, and of a New Covenant to come.[75] Understanding the deeply rooted connection of the Jews with this entire covenantal world helps

---

[74] Deut 28:1-14.

[75] Since the exile from Medo-Persia, the Children of Israel were referred to as Jews since they were of the tribe of Judah. In this work, we use the term "Jews" referring to the old covenant people of God as did the writers of Divine revelation in both the Old and New Testaments. This is not a derogatory or bigoted term, but an historically accepted term to describe the nation of people. For example, in the New King James version of the Bible, the term "Jews" is used 234 times: 68 in the Old Testament and 166 in the New. In the New Revised Standard Version, Catholic Edition, the term "Jews" is used 327 times, 172 times in the Old Testament and 155 times in the New.

us to understand why the Jews would weep intensely at the destruction of the first temple,[76] and again at the destruction of the second temple in A.D. 70.[77]

The Kingdom of Israel Had a Set Number of Days, the Last of Which Would Begin with Christ

Chronological Timeline 2 begins with that point where we first see the term "last days" associated with the Children of Israel. Jacob said to his children, "Gather together, that I may tell you what shall befall you in the *last days*." As we continue to follow passages of Scripture that address the last, or latter days, we see clearly that last days were associated with a finite period of time *associated with Old Testament Israel. Tables 1, 2,* and *3*, and their associated timelines present the prophecies as well as the historic realities of that finite time frame established for the children of Israel until the end of their entire Old Covenant nation, city, and temple.

Chronological Timeline 2 continues with the chronological and relevant events in the Book of Genesis regarding what Jacob said would happen to his sons in those latter days, specifically that a King will come from the tribe of Judah, referred to as Shiloh (a prophecy speaking of Jesus Christ).[78] In the Book of Numbers, a last days prophecy speaks of a Scepter, or King, arising out of Israel with the sign in the heavens of a star, the prophesied star of Bethlehem, which was visible during the birth of Jesus Christ.[79] Finally, Moses adds to these prophesies that eventually the children of Israel would call upon the Lord Jesus after having been scattered to the wind by the Assyrians (722 B.C.) and Babylonians (586 B.C.) for their disobedience.[80]

---

[76] Ezra 3:12.

[77] Rev 1:7.

[78] Gen 49:1, 8-12.

[79] Num. 24:14, 17.

[80] Duet 4:30.

These prophecies prepared the Jews for the Christ to come, who would establish an everlasting Kingdom on earth and assemble His chosen people, the true Jews, from among the Jewish people and the Gentiles, both of whom would believe in Christ so as to make one, holy, catholic, and apostolic people from them. Entrenched, too, in the mind of the Jews was the truth that Christ would bring a change to the redemptive Covenant of Grace by the ratification of a new and better covenant.

One hearing these words of Moses would still require further enlightenment from the prophets to more clearly understand the nature of this coming Christ and His Kingdom. During the days when the twelve tribes entered the Promised Land, the Jews could not imagine that one day after the rebuilding in 516 B.C. of their first temple in Jerusalem after its destruction in 586 B.C., they would have to see the irreparable destruction by fire of their city, its second and final temple, and their redemptive liturgical economy of sacrifices and priesthood due to the nation's persistent apostasy from Yahweh their God.[81]

It is God's revelation—His Word in the Law, the Prophets, and the Writings—that are replete with evidence that this holy covenant nation was to be an expression and type of the coming Kingdom of God on earth. This holy nation of Israel was to bear witness of the righteousness, peace, joy, justice, wisdom, mercy, and love of God to all nations. The children of Israel were to carry on the cultural mandate by obeying God with all of their hearts and loving their neighbors. The Jews knew what they were to do.[82] God told them through Moses: "…this [Law] is your wisdom and your understanding in the sight of the peoples who will hear all these statutes, and say, 'Surely this great nation is a wise

---

[81] One of the more informative authorities on the events of the Last Days of Jerusalem is Joshephus' The Wars of the Jews, written by a Jewish General of Judea who fought for the Jews until his being taken captive by the Romans during the Roman's first century war against Jerusalem. Disgusted with the obstinate rebellion and apostasy of his own people, Josephus aligned his allegiance with the Romans, who surrounded and attacked Jerusalem in A.D. 70 as Jesus Christ prophesied. Flavius Josephus, as one born in Jerusalem and as a Romano-Jewish historian and military leader accurately recorded those events of the Jewish war up to and including the cities complete destruction. He was born to a father of priestly descent.

[82] Luke 10:25-28.

and understanding people. For what great nation is there that has God so near to it, as the Lord our God is to us, for whatever reason we may call upon Him? And what great nation is there that has such statutes and righteous judgments as are in all this law which I set before you this day?'"[83] Jerusalem was to be THE place on earth where the one true God, Yahweh, was worshipped, pointing to a lasting and eternal Kingdom of God that was eternally decreed. But as foretold by the prophets, the first covenant nation was finite and its days numbered. As will be seen in this and subsequent timelines, the prophets and Christ Himself spoke of the *latter days*, the *last days*, and, eventually, the *last hour*[84] associated exclusively with Old Covenant Judea and Jerusalem. The "last days" are not at all speaking of the end of the world as so many misinterpret this term. God knew that many, if not most of His covenant people, the Jews, would fall away from the faith before the latter days of Jerusalem were over. The old world, symbolically called the heavens and earth that then existed, as St. Peter referred to it, would eventually be dissolved, and the new Kingdom, the new King Jesus, and the new holy nation of kings and priests under Christ (the Church, the New Jerusalem) would eventually break forth as prophesied and begin to cover the earth as the waters cover the sea.[85] Proof that this kingdom has come? Consider the celebration of the weekly covenantal communion between Yahweh God and His holy people, the Church of Jesus Christ, in the new feast called the Eucharist as it continues to this day.[86]

---

[83] Deut 4:6-8.

[84] 1 John 2:18.

[85] 2 Pet 3:1-13.

[86] Rev 19:5-9, a picture of the Eucharist now enjoyed by the Church, which is the New Jerusalem having come down from heaven when the Old Jerusalem was taken out of the way (Rev 19:1-3). See the New Heavens and the New Earth, as well as the New Assembly of God's people, the Church of Jesus Christ depicted symbolically in Rev 21-22.

King David's Seed after Him Would Take the Throne of an Everlasting Kingdom

Moving across *Chronological Timeline 2*, around 970 B.C., as Israel's King David was about to die, God made a deeper cut in this unfolding Covenant of Grace that has been called the Davidic Covenant.[87] This covenant adds that Yahweh God will raise up from David's lineage a King who would build a house for Israel, a dwelling place of God. God adds that this King's kingdom would last forever. The faithful among the children of Israel would now look forward in faith to a Messiah (translated into Greek as *Christos*) who saves, a Prophet who speaks God's Words, a Priest according to the Order of Melchizedek, and a King who would rule over God's Kingdom forever. Redemptive history tells us that his natural son and heir, Solomon (also called Jedidiah by the prophet, Nathan), would not be the complete fulfillment of all of this prophecy to David. The complete fulfillment of One who would be Prophet, Priest, and King, and who would build a Church in which God would dwell by His Spirit would be Jesus Christ alone. Solomon, however, the wisest of all men and a man of peace, was appointed by God to build the first temple in which God would dwell. This Davidic Covenant as part of the Covenant of Grace completes the entire covenantal and kingdom enterprise that was to be a type and shadow of the Kingdom of God to come in Jesus Christ, who, like Solomon, was of the Seed of David and Abraham.

The Prophesied Messiah King, Jesus, Would Suffer Before Reigning and Conquering

We now turn to the prophets who wrote 300-700 years prior to Christ Jesus' birth. They spoke of the Messiah King to come in the form of the Servant of Yahweh (usually translated as Servant of the LORD) born from the lineage of

---

[87] 2 Sam 7:12-17.

David, which is why He is referred to as the "Son of David".[88] Isaiah said that the Servant of Yahweh would be born of a Virgin and would come to His people humbly on a donkey into Jerusalem. The Christ would bring resurrection life to Jerusalem, to Zion, and to the entire covenant nation.[89] He would resuscitate the spiritual life of God's people who were likened unto, as Ezekiel saw the nation, a valley of dry bones who come to life. The coming Christ, although presented as a coming King would arrive as a humble Servant and give His life as a ransom for the sins of many.[90] We now learn that the coming Messiah will have a salvific ministry to put an end to the power of original and subsequent sin by becoming the sacrificial Lamb of God whose innocent blood would efficaciously cleanse the souls of men (hence, the Christ being called the "suffering" Servant of Yahweh).[91]

This aspect of the Messiah King is what many of the Jews failed to see in the obedience of Christ Jesus due to their hardness of heart. The unbelieving rulers of the Jews, however, could not deny Jesus' miracle of raising a dead man, Lazarus, to life, and they were concerned that everyone would believe in Jesus resulting in the Roman authorities taking away their positions of rulership and their place as a nation. It is worth noting the words of the high priest when the Jews were upset over Jesus' miracles, the people's faith in Him, and the threat of losing their high positions: "And one of them, Caiaphas, being high priest that year, said to them, 'You know nothing at all, nor do you consider that it is expedient for us that one man should die for the people, and not that the whole nation should perish.' Now this he did not say on his own authority; but being high priest that year he prophesied that Jesus would die for the nation, and not for that nation only, but also that He would gather together in one the children of God who were scattered abroad. Then, from that day on, they plotted to put Him to death."[92] On the other hand, the humble, those who had been born of the Spirit, born again, or born from above remembered the words of Isaiah who

---

[88] Ps(s) 2, 110, 42.

[89] Ezek 37:5-14.

[90] C.f., Phil 2:5-11.

[91] Isa 2, 42, and 53.

[92] John 11:49-53.

spoke of the Servant who would die for the sins of the nation before being exalted to restore the Kingdom to the New Israel:

"For He shall grow up before Him as a tender plant, and as a root out of dry ground. He has no form or comeliness; and when we see Him, there is no beauty that we should desire Him. He is despised and rejected by men, a Man of sorrows and acquainted with grief. And we hid, as it were, our faces from Him; He was despised, and we did not esteem Him. Surely He has borne our griefs and carried our sorrows; yet we esteemed Him stricken, smitten by God, and afflicted. But He was wounded for our transgressions, He was bruised for our iniquities; the chastisement for our peace was upon Him, and by His stripes we are healed. All we like sheep have gone astray; we have turned, every one, to his own way; and the Lord has laid on Him the iniquity of us all. He was oppressed and He was afflicted, yet He opened not His mouth; He was led as a lamb to the slaughter, and as a sheep before its shearers is silent, so He opened not His mouth. He was taken from prison and from judgment, and who will declare His generation? For He was cut off from the land of the living; for the transgressions of My people He was stricken. And they made His grave with the wicked—but with the rich at His death, because He had done no violence, nor was any deceit in His mouth. Yet it pleased the Lord to bruise Him; He has put Him to grief. When You make His soul an offering for sin, He shall see His seed, He shall prolong His days, and the pleasure of the Lord shall prosper in His hand. He shall see the labor of His soul, and be satisfied. By His knowledge My righteous Servant shall justify many, for He shall bear their iniquities. Therefore I will divide Him a portion with the great, and He shall divide the spoil with the strong, because He poured out His soul unto death, and He was numbered with the transgressors, and He bore the sin of many, and made intercession for the transgressors.[93]

The First Covenant Promised a New Covenant and a New Heavens and New Earth

Looking at *Chronological Timeline 2*, after learning from Yahweh God through the prophets that Messiah would be a King who would first suffer for the sins of the covenant people, we see that God then prepares His people through those same prophets for a New Covenant with better promises than the Old Covenant, and for a New Heavens and New Earth. During the days of the first covenant ratified on Mt. Sinai, the prophets placed into the hearts of the church of the Old Covenant the truth that Yahweh God would make a new covenant with them, which meant giving them a new heart, a fleshy heart upon which His holy laws would be written, and in which His Holy Spirit would dwell, causing the people to obey His words and walk in His ways. This promise of Yahweh's New Covenant is perfectly and beautifully tied to the fulfillment of the promises of the cultural mandate, the blessings promised to Abraham, and the divine promise of the perpetual Kingdom given to Israel's son, Judah, and to David's lineage. This new covenant, its New Jerusalem, its new temple, and its new people would be realized in the last days of the Old Covenant Jerusalem, its temple, and its people.

These last days were synonymous with the coming of Christ Jesus as High Priest and His Kingdom, which would also usher in the eventual abolition of the Old Testament order as the writer to the Hebrews has recorded:

> "Now this is the main point of the things we are saying: We have such a High Priest, who is seated at the right hand of the throne of the Majesty in the heavens, a Minister of the sanctuary and of the true tabernacle which the Lord erected, and not man. For every high priest is appointed to offer both gifts

---

[93] Is 53:2-12; c.f., 1 Peter 2:18-24.

and sacrifices. Therefore, it is necessary that this One also have something to offer. For if He were on earth, He would not be a priest, since there are priests who offer the gifts according to the law; who serve the copy and shadow of the heavenly things, as Moses was divinely instructed when he was about to make the tabernacle. For He said, "See that you make all things according to the pattern shown you on the mountain." But now He has obtained a more excellent ministry, inasmuch as He is also Mediator of a better covenant, which was established on better promises. For if that first covenant had been faultless, then no place would have been sought for a second. Because finding fault with them, He says: "Behold, the days are coming, says the Lord, when I will make a new covenant with the house of Israel and with the house of Judah— not according to the covenant that I made with their fathers in the day when I took them by the hand to lead them out of the land of Egypt; because they did not continue in My covenant, and I disregarded them," says the Lord. "For this is the covenant that I will make with the house of Israel after those days," says the Lord: "I will put My laws in their mind and write them on their hearts; and I will be their God, and they shall be My people. None of them shall teach his neighbor, and none his brother, saying, 'Know the Lord,' for all shall know Me, from the least of them to the greatest of them. For I will be merciful to their unrighteousness, and their sins and their lawless deeds I will remember no more." In that He says, "A new covenant," He has made the first obsolete. Now what is becoming obsolete and growing old is ready to vanish away.[94]

By the time of the sixth century B.C., the entire Old Covenant order, referred to above as the entire heavens and earth to the Jew, was beginning to be spoken of as something that would in the future be abolished to make way for the New Covenant. One could say that the Old Covenant was a sort of scaffolding erected

---

[94] Heb 8:1-15.

to support the building of the New Jerusalem, the Church, and the Kingdom of God. The prophets of old—Isaiah, Ezekiel, Micah—as well as the apostles of the New Covenant age—St. Peter and St. John—prophesied of this New Heavens and New Earth, which included a canvas of features associated with its inauguration, its progressive growth, and its final consummation prior to the Final Judgment (or what the Church has referred to as the "Second Coming" or "Return of Christ").[95]

The reflections of this work make a distinction between the coming of Christ in salvation and judgment in A.D. 70, and that of the final, or Second Coming of Christ at the end of this current age of the growth of Christ's Kingdom. Old Covenant Israel, its city of Jerusalem in the Middle East, its temple, its priesthood and redemptive sacrifices are clearly presented in the New Testament, especially in the Epistle to the Hebrews, as temporal and designed to point to the covenantal fulfillment and spiritual and eternal reality of Christ Jesus, the Prophet, High Priest, and King, as well as His Kingdom to come. The features of the New Heavens and New Earth that would progressively be realized in time and on earth beginning with the coming of Christ would be the following:

- Justice, righteousness, peace abounding in the earth

- Peoples of every nation, tribe, and language rejoicing and walking in the light of God's Law

- Through the Spirit of God, the Law of God being placed into the hearts of men to know and do God's will

- Deserts blooming like a rose

- All nations coming to worship the King Christ

- Weapons of war over time being turned to implements of production, and war being learned no more

- Every man and his descendants being blessed

---

[95] Isa 65:17; Ezek 43-48; Mic 4; 2 Pet 3:13; Rev 21:22-22:11.

- Zion, the New Jerusalem being the dwelling place of God

- Whole world being holy, not just the "Holy Land" in the Middle East

The Old Testament believers believed and obeyed the words of John the Baptizer, repented of their sins, were baptized with a baptism of repentance, believed in the Christ to come, and were then baptized in the name of the Father, Son, and Holy Spirit. These faithful saints then believed the teachings of Jesus and His apostles that the last days were upon them, so they began looking forward to the New Heavens and New Earth and the coming of Christ and His Kingdom. They recognized they were living in the last days of the Old Covenant and that Christ was really coming soon. Yet, how were so many actually prepared for the coming of the Messiah and the coming end of the Old Testament age? We can thank the prophet Daniel for providing us with the details regarding the last days and what and when they really were.

TABLE 2. THE PROPHET DANIEL'S "70 WEEKS" FORETELLS ISRAEL'S END AND THE KINGDOM OF GOD'S BEGINNING

A pivotal passage of Sacred Scripture that lays the foundation for our understanding of the term "last days" and even provides a timeline for the numbered days of Israel can be found in the Book of the Prophet Daniel. This eschatological passage in Daniel, Chapter 9:20-27, to which we dedicate *Table 2* and *Chronological Timeline 3*, presents what theologians have titled "Daniel's 70 Weeks." In this passage, Daniel hears from the Archangel Gabriel what will happen to the people of God from the time they depart from the captivity of the Medo-Persians until the end of the Old Covenant nation itself, also known as the "end of the age." This "70 Weeks" prophecy is part of Daniel's series of writings that take place from the second year of King Nebuchadnezzar (about 584 B.C) through the reign of Darius of the Medes, who ruled over the Medo-Persian empire (about 537 B.C.). This prophecy depicts God's Kingdom of Israel as it existed among and related to the Babylonian, Medo-Persian, Greek (or Hellenistic), and finally the Roman kingdoms or empires. *Table 3* and its *Chronological Timeline 4* elaborate specifically on these relationships. As to the interpretation of the term "70 weeks," theologians who interpret this passage from the standpoint of a historic Hebrew understanding of the term "weeks" in this context, would declare that Daniel is speaking of 70 seven-year cycles, or 70 sevens, as translated in the Septuagint (the Greek translation of the Old Testament). Why seven-year cycles? Because a "week," or seven-year cycle, is the normal cycle of time within the Jewish community, which ends with the Year of Release when all debts are forgiven. Therefore, Daniel is saying that 70 seven-year cycles, or 490 years, are appointed for God's covenant people, the Jews, and their holy city of Jerusalem, the city of the Great King. Daniel received this prophecy while the nation of Judah was in captivity in Babylon by King Nebuchadnezzar, which began in 586 B.C, seen as the first point on timeline 3. King Darius of the Medes eventually conquered Babylon in 539 B.C., and

Daniel most likely prophesied during those first few years of the Medo-Persian empire ruled by Darius, son of Ahasuerus. Daniel's prophecies build upon *Chronological Timelines 1 and 2*, and they point and allude to the last days of Old Covenant Israel.[96] The term "Last Days," and "Latter Days," spoken of today in theological, religious, historical, and social circles come primarily from these passages in the Book of Daniel, although they throw the timeline of these *then* days out into our future. Here is an exposition of the notable portions of this famous and prophetic passage, which we will now analyze verse-by-verse.

Daniel 9:24 "Seventy weeks are determined for your people and for your holy city, to finish the transgression, to make an end of sins, to make reconciliation for iniquity, to bring in everlasting righteousness, to seal up vision and prophecy, and to anoint the Most Holy.

God was faithful to Daniel, a righteous man, to bring prophetic vision and understanding to him regarding what would become of the Jews at the end of their nation's days.[97] In this 70 Weeks vision, St. Gabriel informed Daniel that his people and the holy city of Jerusalem have 490 years remaining in which six redemptive acts will occur. As stated earlier, the 70 weeks is equal to 70 seven-year cycles (known figuratively as weeks), which equaled a total of 490 years. It must be understood here that the 490 years, although having a definitive beginning, as we will see, and an assured end, *do not occur consecutively from beginning to end.* We will note *a pause* during the "last week," the 70th week, which is what causes the mystery, which we will examine. We can note with assurance that within those 490 years, the transgression of Adam will be finished, the power of sins will be ended, reconciliation between God and man will be made, and everlasting righteousness and eternal life will be ushered in. Also, God's prophetic, public, and direct revelation for His people will be complete, and the Most Holy in the heavens (God's heavenly dwelling place) will be anointed, of which the Jerusalem temple was a type and shadow.

---

[96] Dan 2:28; 8:19, 23; 10:14.

[97] Dan 9:22-23, c.f., Dan 12:8.

Interpreting this passage from the vantage point of the 21st century of redemptive history while taking advantage of all the Church has learned of Christ this side of the cross in the past 2000 years, we know that Jesus, Daniel's Messiah Prince, or the Anointed One, the Christ, through His humility and obedience to, and suffering for the will of God, made atonement for and an end of transgressions and reconciled God's people to Himself from both the Jews and the Gentiles making them one in Christ Jesus.

Christ Jesus ushered in an everlasting righteousness by His vanquishing death and the power of original sin brought to mankind by Adam. Jesus destroyed the power of death and the devil forever and set mankind free from the devil's deception, oppression, and possession. As it is written, "Since the children have flesh and blood, [He] too shared in their humanity so that by his death he might break the power of him who holds the power of death—that is, the devil—and free those who all their lives were held in slavery by their fear of death."[98] This is significant, especially as we talk of the binding of Satan by King Jesus at the end of the 70 weeks. Nonetheless, this is a process that has *definitive* markers, *progressive* development and growth over time, and a *final* ending.

---

[98] Heb 2:14-15.

Table 2. The Prophet Daniel's "70 Weeks" Foretells Israel's End and the Kingdom of God's Beginning

Final 3 ½ years of the Last Week is the Great Tribulation of which Daniel and Jesus spoke. C.f., Matt 23, 24, 25, having occurred between A.D. 66-70.

490th Year

1st of Tishri, A.D. 70
Jerusalem, its temple, its redemptive system, its priesthood were all destroyed forever. Israel's entire heaven & earth were destroyed by fire in A.D. 70.

First 3 ½ years of the Last Week

490 years (70 * 7 weeks of years)

483 years (69 * 7 weeks of years)

Chronological Timeline

586 B.C. Babylon takes Jerusalem captive for 70 years. Daniel prophesies while in Babylon about the covenant people Israel's last days and the New Kingdom.

457 B.C. Ezra receives the decree to go to Jerusalem, and dedicates the rebuilt temple.

444 B.C. Wall around the city of Jerusalem rebuilt by Nehemiah.

A.D. 26-30 Jesus Christ Begins His ministry. Concludes with His making a New Covenant with His people, and getting cut off/murdered by the unbelieving Jews.

40 yrs
A.D. 30 – AD 70

40 yr. period where the Church wandered faithfully in the wilderness until the Lord's appearing, or His Parousia, to save her, bring refreshing, execute judgment on her enemies, and gather her together, Rev 12.

A.D. 26   A.D. 70

The **Last Days, or Latter Days** in Scripture refer to the last days of Old Covenant Israel and Jerusalem. Begins with Jesus' ministry and ends with the fall of Jerusalem in A.D. 70. Heb 1 / Matt 23:37-39.

The Components of Daniels 70 Weeks Prophecy, Dan 9:20-27.

- 70 weeks (70 7-year cycles) = 490 years are determined for the Jews & Jerusalem From the commandment to restore Jerusalem to the Anointed One, a Prince, there will be 7 weeks and 62 weeks (69 weeks)
- To end sin, make reconciliation for sinners
- To bring in everlasting righteousness
- To seal vision, revelation from God
- To anoint the Most Holy in heaven
- 69 of these weeks between Ezra getting the decree from God to build Jerusalem and its wall, and Messiah's appearance in AD 26. Jesus was born about 4 B.C.
- After the 69 weeks (483 yrs), 1 final week of 7 years remains. In the first 3 ½ years of the final week (from A.D. 26-A.D. 30, the ministry of Christ/Messiah begins and then ends with His crucifixion. He brings an end to sacrifice and offering.

- In the last 3.5 years of the last 7 weeks of years, which was the unknown portion of Daniel's 70 weeks, the Prince of the Romans (Caesar) will destroy the city and bring abomination that shall make desolate. Jerusalem was destroyed and the First Covenant completely abrogated in AD 70.

Matt 24 2 And Jesus said to them, "Do you not see all these things? Assuredly, I say to you, not one stone shall be left here upon another, that shall not be thrown down." 3 Now as He sat on the Mount of Olives, the disciples came to Him privately, saying, "Tell us, when will these things be? And what will be the sign of Your coming, and of the end of the age?"

Matt 21: 43 "Therefore I say to you, the kingdom of God will be taken from you and given to a nation bearing the fruits of it. 44 And whoever falls on this stone will be broken; but on whomever it falls, it will grind him to powder."

After Jesus Christ's resurrection from the dead, He ascended to Heaven and gave apostles, prophets, evangelists, pastors, and teachers to His Church, the New Jerusalem, to preach and teach of the Gospel of the Kingdom. They did so in all the Roman world as a witness prior to the destruction of the city of Jerusalem and the crushing of Jerusalem by the Romans. The sealing of prophetic vision and revelation came in the first century as Jesus Christ was given a final revelation of Himself, the Revelation of Jesus Christ (that is the Book of the Revelation), *which was given to Him by God His Father*, which was then given by Jesus to St. John, who recorded this revelation in what is now the last book of the Bible included in the Canon of Sacred Scripture. This final revelation from God was the sealing of direct revelation, thus bringing an end to prophetic revelation as Daniel recorded. With the giving of the Revelation of Jesus Christ, the Church would now become the steward of the complete and public Revelation of Jesus Christ.[99]

Finally, regarding the anointing of the Most Holy, upon Christ's entrance into His Lordship in heaven after His resurrection,[100] He, as High Priest, anointed the Holiest Place in the heavens, God's dwelling place, with His own blood. All these things occurred within the 490 years determined for Daniel's people. We now look at when the doomsday clock for the Old Covenant, the City of Jerusalem, its temple, and its people would start ticking, and when the ticking would end with the city left desolate.

---

[99] Christianity—a revealed religion—works with two different kinds of revelation. The revelation that came to us from Christ, through the prophets before him and the apostles after, is an unchanged body of teachings called the "deposit of faith," and it is considered by the Church as public revelation, so called because Christ said it was to be given to all nations. It's the substance of our religion. Public revelation is closed within the canon of Sacred Scripture of the Old and New Testaments. Everything that God needed to reveal about Christianity already has been revealed, so nothing needs to be added; Christ himself revealed it, so nothing has to be changed...Vatican II repeated, "as the new and definitive covenant, will never pass away, and we now await no further new public revelation before the glorious manifestation of our Lord Jesus Christ." Phenomena such as apparitions or prophetic utterances since the first century are considered "private revelations," and although some private revelations may be accepted as authentic by the Church, they are not considered binding upon the Church to believe and obey. Catholic Answers, https://www.catholic.com/magazine/online-edition/the-ten-most-common-misconceptions-about-apparitions

[100] Mark 16:19.

25 "Know therefore and understand, that from the going forth of the command to restore and build Jerusalem until Messiah the Prince, there shall be seven weeks and sixty-two weeks; the street shall be built again, and the wall, even in troublesome times.

Noting *Chronological Timeline 3*, the countdown of the 490 years until Jerusalem's end begins with Ezra's receiving the decree to go to Jerusalem to dedicate its rebuilt temple. Dan 9:25 provides the initial insight that the first 69 weeks literally recorded as "seven plus 62 weeks" of the 70 weeks of years, totaling 483 of the 490 years, would bring mankind to the day of the Christ, Messiah the Prince, the King of the Kingdom of God. The 483 years from the command to Ezra would bring us to the ministry, not the birth, of Jesus Christ. The fulfilment of this "command to restore and build the city" came through the decree spoken by King Artaxerxes to Ezra the priest.[101] The temple had been rebuilt by 516 B.C., and it was eventually dedicated by Ezra by this decree around 516 to 515 B.C., soon before the Passover Feast. One's read of the books of Ezra and Nehemiah reveals that the Jerusalem temple and the wall of the city, which were destroyed by the Babylonians in 586 B.C., were indeed rebuilt in troublesome times. God gave grace as He sent prophets to encourage the people in their building. Zechariah's and Haggai's prophetic books record this encouragement to build. Nehemiah said himself that the joy of the Lord would be their strength as they guarded the wall with a weapon in one hand and with implements to build the wall in the other. Nehemiah led the building of the wall to its completion in 444 B.C.

According to Daniel's prophecy, 483 years from 457 B.C. would bring us to A.D. 26. This was when the Messiah Jesus, the Prince of God, began his ministry in Galilee by preaching the Gospel of the Kingdom, teaching and healing all who were oppressed by the devil. Knowing that the Messiah would come forth during this time frame, the wise men from Persia, known as the Magi, would have been keenly aware of this and other prophecies concerning the coming Christ. They could have counted backwards around 30 years, noted the Star of Bethlehem in the East, and discerned the time frame of Jesus' birth. The Magi would then arrive

---

[101] Ezra 7:11-26.

in Jerusalem at the house in which Joseph and Mary were staying to visit the "young Child" Jesus, sometime after his birth, but before His second birthday.

26 "And after the sixty-two weeks Messiah shall be cut off, but not for Himself; and the people of the prince who is to come shall destroy the city and the sanctuary. The end of it shall be with a flood, and till the end of the war desolations are determined.

Continuing from the beginning of the public ministry of Messiah Jesus in A.D. 26, where the first 69 weeks ended, we learn from St. Gabriel that the Christ will be cut off, or destroyed, or murdered, with the qualifying phrase, "but not for Himself," which we now know is a reference to Jesus Christ's being, as Isaiah prophesied, "cut off" from the land of the living to satisfy the penalty for the transgressions of His people.[102] This passage also looks ahead to the Days of Vengeance that would come upon the city of Jerusalem and its temple by the Romans through General Titus Caesar Vespasianus under the authority of his father, Emperor Titus Flavius Vespasianus, in A.D. 70.[103] We also see a reference to the future Jewish war, as Josephus called it, which began with the Jews cutting off the daily sacrifices for the emperor, which greatly angered Caesar Nero, and which eventually concluded with the Romans surrounding Jerusalem, destroying its temple, burning and leveling both to the ground, and either murdering or enslaving its inhabitants. The conflagration of the great city of Jerusalem was completed with the captivity of those who survived the city's siege. Daniel called this time period between A.D. 66 and A.D. 70, "a flood" and an appointment with desolation, as some translations appropriately put it. This time frame was what was described by Jesus as a time of great and unprecedented tribulation and distress,[104] or as St. Paul referred to it, the "great distress"[105] during which all those things prophesied by Jesus against apostate Jerusalem would come to pass.[106] The generation to which Jesus referred as perverted and faithless was the one

---

[102] Isa 53:3-11.

[103] Luke 21:20-22.

[104] Matt 24:21; Mark 13:19, 24.

[105] 1 Cor 7:26; Rom. 8:35.

[106] Matt 23:36; 24:34.

then living during the days of Jesus' preaching and speaking those words. That generation would be that "terminal generation" who would see the coming of the Lord to bring salvation to His people and vengeance upon those who rejected Him and who persecuted, ostracized, and murdered His New Covenant people, the Christians consisting of both converted Jews and Gentiles. That terminal generation would see the desolation of Jerusalem and its sanctuary the temple, referred to by St. John in the Revelation of Jesus Christ as Babylon, the Great Whore, who was filled with abominable behaviors, ethical filthiness, and the sins of fornicating with the Roman world against Yahweh God and His Christ.[107]

27 Then he shall confirm a covenant with many for one week; but in the middle of the week He shall bring an end to sacrifice and offering. And on the wing of abominations shall be one who makes desolate, even until the consummation, which is determined, is poured out on the desolate."

We now come to the 70th week, the final seven-year cycle which began with the ministry of Jesus and ends with Jerusalem's desolation. How does that occur if Jesus' ministry began in A.D. 26, and the destruction of Jerusalem occurred in A.D. 70, in between which is a period of 44 years? I propose that the 70th week is broken into two 3 ½-year periods that are divided by Messiah's being cut off, or in other words, His Crucifixion. *Chronological Timeline 5* depicts these two 3 ½ year periods as: 1) Jesus' ministry between A.D. 26, and A.D. 30, totaling 3 ½ years, and 2) the Great Tribulation between A.D. 66, and A.D. 70, totaling 3 ½ years. The sum of both periods equal the last week of seven years, even though the two periods were separated by about 37 years.

Jesus ministered for 3 ½ years from beginning in Cana of Galilee until His death on the cross on Good Friday outside of the city of Jerusalem in A.D. 30. Prior to His death, Jesus affirmed the New Covenant with His chosen disciples

---

[107] Apostate Jerusalem is presented in the Revelation of Jesus Christ as Mystery, Babylon the Great, The Mother of Harlots and of the Abominations of the Earth in Rev 17-19. Note how in Rev 17, she is clothed with precious stones, but she is a liar and is doomed to destruction by the Lord's appearing. Also note, that the Church of Jesus Christ, the New Jerusalem, is made up of similar precious stones and is arrayed as a pure and holy bride, who has prepared herself for her marriage to the King, Christ Jesus, and for her partaking with Him of the Marriage Supper of the Lamb, which we now call the Eucharist.

and to all those who would believe by instituting what we now know as the Eucharist, the Lord's Supper, "this cup is the New Covenant in My blood, which is shed for you."[108] Afterwards, by virtue of His completed work on the cross, Jesus Christ brought an end to Old Testament redemptive sacrifice and offering forever as Daniel prophesied. The writer to the Hebrew Christians wrote, "And every priest stands ministering daily and offering repeatedly the same sacrifices, which can never take away sins. But this Man, after He had offered one sacrifice for sins forever, sat down at the right hand of God, from that time waiting till His enemies are made His footstool.[109]

For a season between A.D. 30 and A.D. 70, the temple sacrifices and offerings would continue as part of those things which could be shaken, until the time would come in A.D. 70, when the old heavens and earth of the Old Covenant would be shaken to the ground and forever, vanquished and forgotten. As the writer to the Hebrews warned his converted Jewish audience:

> "See that you do not refuse Him who speaks. For if they did not escape who refused Him who spoke on earth, much more shall we not escape if we turn away from Him who speaks from heaven, whose voice then shook the earth; but now He has promised, saying, "Yet once more I shake not only the earth, but also heaven." Now this, "Yet once more," indicates the removal of those things that are being shaken, as of things that are made, that the things which cannot be shaken may remain. Therefore, since we are receiving a kingdom which cannot be shaken, let us have grace, by which we may serve God acceptably with reverence and godly fear. For our God is a consuming fire.[110]

Those ceremonial, or redemptive laws which were but a type and shadow of the eternal reality to come in Christ Jesus were abrogated definitively at the cross

---

[108] Luke 22:20.

[109] Heb 10:11-13.

[110] Heb 12:25-29.

and would be completely passed away just 40 years later. In fact, the 40-year time span in between the Resurrection and Ascension of Christ until the destruction of the City and temple by the Romans were referred to as the time of the Church's "wandering in the wilderness" while being fed by God and while being tested until her coming into the Lord's Kingdom at His Appearing, His Parousia, at the end of this 40-year period. This time strikingly corresponded to the forty years of testing of the Old Covenant assembly in the desert of Sinai, and Jesus's 40-day testing in the desert outside of Galilee, and the Church's trial during the first century depicted symbolically as the Woman's fleeing to the desert as presented in Rev 12. From our 21st century vantage point looking back upon the events of the first century, we note that the Lord sustained the Woman, His young and fledgling Church, and kept Her safe until the end of the age, namely the Old Testament age.[111] The King of the Kingdom of God, Jesus, protected and gave the Woman, His Church, a place prepared by God for 3 ½ years (1260 days).[112] Here is the mystery: We know that after Jesus' Death and Resurrection, a Great Tribulation would come that would last 3 ½ years, which is the last half of the final 70th week of Daniel's 70 weeks prophecy. Neither Christ's disciples nor even Jesus Himself knew when that last 3 ½ years would occur. It was a mystery until God, the Father, would reveal that day and hour to Jesus in the Revelation of Jesus Christ as previously mentioned.

Today, both historians and a growing number of theologians see this text in Daniel as depicting the destruction of Jerusalem and its temple in A.D. 70.[113] When one looks at the rest of the Book of Daniel, chapters 10-12, one notes a description of what happens to the House of Israel from the days of Cyrus king of Persia through the days of the Roman Emperor Vespasian, whose son attacked the Holy City of Jerusalem, sacked it, and burned its temple to the ground, "leaving not one stone left upon another," as Jesus prophesied. Titus' soldiers entered the temple's holiest place with their idolatrous eagle ensigns, which were a symbol of emperor and state worship, thus being an abomination that desecrated the holy

---

[111] Rev 12:5-6.

[112] Ibid.

[113] Matt 23:37-38.

temple and made it desolate. This occurred on the first of the month of Tishri in A.D. 70. It is interesting that on that the same day in 586 B.C., the soldiers of King Nebuchadnezzar of Babylon attacked the city of Jerusalem and destroyed the first temple, Solomon's temple. In Daniel Chapter 12, we see that prior to the end of the city and temple, when all of the power of the holy people should be completely shattered, and prior to all of these prophecies coming to pass, there will be a time of great trouble, called the "Great Tribulation" that would take place during the final 3 ½ years of Daniel's 70 weeks.[114] As mentioned earlier, Josephus wrote of those historical events leading up to the destruction of Jerusalem in his The Wars of the Jews. (One can also read much about these events that occurred during the first century Great Tribulation in selections from the "Sources List" at the end of this book. *This* was the Great Tribulation prior to A.D. 70, prophesied by Jesus and St. John,[115] during which Caesar Nero was, what the Scriptures referred to as, "the man of sin (lawlessness), the son of perdition,[116] whose number was 666,"[117] the one who was Antichrist. The mystery is cleared when one sees a break in the last, or 70th, week, thus separating the ministry of Christ from the beginning of the Great Tribulation. Daniel wanted to understand when this end of the Holy City of earthly Jerusalem would be.[118] The disciples asked the same question, to which Jesus prophesied about the end of the Old Covenant Age, which would include the distress upon the whole Roman world that would climax into a 3 ½ year Great Tribulation, which would end with the destruction of Jerusalem and its temple, all of which would be the end of the holy people,[119] the conflagration of THEIR entire heavens and earth, not ours.[120] However, the good news and the hope that anchored the soul of the New Testament Church at that time was that the end of the Old Covenant

---

[114] Dan 12:7.

[115] Matt 23-25; Mark 12-13; Luke 19-21, Rev 1-20:6.

[116] 2 Thess 2:2-4.

[117] Rev 13:18.

[118] Dan 12:8-9.

[119] Dan 12:1, 7.

[120] 2Pet. 3:10-14.

elements would mean the glorious and powerful inauguration of the Kingdom of God having come in power,[121] which the Church now enjoys today. We enjoy our habitation in this Church of the Living God, a New Jerusalem born out of heaven, the New Testament Church, the dwelling place of God, Zion, and a New Heavens and New Earth, all of which simultaneously came definitively in A.D. 70. This end of the old and beginning of the new on the first of Tishri A.D. 70, also marked the time, as Jesus Christ the King spoke, when the Kingdom of God was taken from the Jewish nation of the First Covenant and was given to the Church of the New Covenant, consisting of converted Jews and the Gentiles, who would bear fruit worthy of the Kingdom.[122] Those believers who heard these prophesies of Daniel and who added faith to their hearing, feared God and sought His favor in doing good while awaiting the Christ to come.

---

[121] Matt 16:28; Mark 9:1; Luke 9:27.

[122] Matt 21:43.

TABLE 3. DANIEL'S PROPHECIES OF THE KINGDOM OF GOD AMONG THE WORLD'S GREAT KINGDOMS

Just as our early Church fathers placed the name of Pontius Pilate, the fifth governor of the Roman province of Judea, serving under Emperor Tiberius from 26-27 A.D. to 36-37 A.D., into the Apostle's Creed to depict Jesus' crucifixion under a real historic figure, the prophet Daniel, as depicted in *Table 3*, *Chronological Timeline 4*, presents the estate of Judea, Jerusalem, and the Jews during the rise and fall of the primary kingdoms of the world.[123] Daniel's book presents an affirmation of history and what would become of the Jewish nation and those nations among whom she lived. Daniel's prophesies gave the House of Israel hope and moral guidance during the rise and fall of the kingdoms of Babylon, Medo-Persia, Greece, and Rome. From our vantage point today looking back, we clearly see Daniel's prophesies as being fulfilled as they spoke of the happenings of the holy people during Daniel's time in the sixth century B.C., through the prophesied events that would occur between Daniel's days and those of the first century A.D.

In this section of redemptive history, one would see the Kingdom of the Jews during the days of the Persian kings, the heroics of the Maccabees during the days of Antiochus Epiphanes, the rise of the Roman emperors, the coming of Messiah Jesus, the first century growth of Christ's Church, the Great Tribulation of A.D. 66-70, the destruction of Jerusalem and its temple desolation, and the vindication of Christ and His holy people, the Christian Church. In addition, one would see in Daniel's book the last days of the earthly Jerusalem and her end, as well as the resurrection of the just ones of both the old and the new Israel. One also sees in Daniel's prophesies the continuing growth of the Kingdom of God and Christ's Church, the Mountain of the Lord's House, as it was prophesied as covering the entire earth with Christ Jesus as the reigning King and Lord over all.

---

[123] Dan 2:36-45; 7:1-28; 12:1-13.

Table 3: Daniel Sees God's Use of Historic Kingdoms to Prepare for the Coming Christ

Dan 2:36-45; 7:1-28; 12:1-13.

Chronological Timeline

The Kingdom of God rules over all these great kingdoms from heaven.   The lesson from Daniel 4:"...the Most High rules in the kingdom of men...For His

God sustains Old Testament Israel during the rule of these world kingdoms.   dominion is an everlasting dominion and His kingdom is from generation to generation."

Kingdom 1
Babylon in 586 B.C.
- Statue's gold head
- Lion/eagle's wings
- Wings plucked, and image stood like a man, and given a man's heart (Nebuchadnezzar)

Kingdom 2
Medo-Persia in 539 B.C.
- Takes Babylon, but inferior
- Chest and arms of the image are silver
- The Bear, devouring the world

Kingdom 3
Greece in 330 B.C.
- Takes Persia
- Belly and thigh of the image is bronze
- The leopard
- 4 heads: Alexander's generals
- Dominion given by God to it

Kingdom 4
Rome in 63 B.C.
- Takes Greece
- Is the last great Kingdom
- Iron kingdom, dreadful, terrible
- Exceedingly strong, fills the entire known earth
- Legs of iron, and iron teeth
- 10 Horns are 10 provinces, or 10 Caesars
- Emperor Nero speaking pompous words, but will go to perdition
- Will break in pieces and crush all other kingdoms

Kingdom 5
Roman Alliance with Apostate Jerusalem
- Iron mixed with clay (Israel was the clay in God, the Potter's hands)
- Eventually, in the latter days, Rome would mix with apostate Israel against Christ and His people. Ps(s) 2, Rev 13.

Last Kingdom
The Kingdom of God
- Jesus preached this Kingdom in A.D. 26
- Shall break in pieces and shall stand forever
- Comes initially as the little Stone, Christ
- Comes in power in A.D. 70

Throughout Redemptive and World History, God's Kingdom of Israel Was a Type and Shadow of the Kingdom of Christ That Would Come.
The Heavenly Kingdom Comes Forth, and the Earthly Israel Is Shaken to Pieces.

The Final Shaking of the Heavens and Earth as the Old Testament Order: the entire heavens and earth to the Jewish nation, comes down like a scaffolding, as Christ's Kingdom, the New Covenant Order breaks forth and covers the earth, thus, an inauguration of the New Heavens and New Earth.

Heb 12: 26 "Yet once more I will shake not only the earth but also the heaven." 27 This phrase, "Yet once more," indicates the removal of what is shaken, as of what has been made, in order that what cannot be shaken may remain. 28 Therefore let us be grateful for receiving a kingdom that cannot be shaken, and thus let us offer to God acceptable worship, with reverence and awe; 29 for our God is a consuming fire.

The Kingdoms with Which the Covenant People Would Interface until the Coming of Messiah

Blessed Daniel the prophet received tremendous insights regarding the Kingdom of God and the last days of His people, the Jews. As Daniel was taken captive by the Babylonians around 586 B.C., he was called upon to interpret King Nebuchadnezzar's dream, in which the king saw a great image whose component body parts represented the Babylonian Kingdom as well as those kingdoms that would arise in the world after Babylon's fall.[124] In that dream, Daniel tells King Nebuchadnezzar that he and his kingdom of Babylon (Kingdom 1 in *Table 3*) were the golden head of that image. Daniel then explains to the king that another kingdom would come after him, the Medo-Persian Kingdom (Kingdom 2 in 539 B.C.), which would be inferior to Nebuchadnezzar's kingdom. The Medo-Persian Kingdom would give way to the Kingdom of Greece (Kingdom 3 in 330 B.C.), which would rule over the earth, being the kingdom led by King Philip II of Macedonia and his son Alexander the Great, after whose death the Grecian Kingdom would be succeeded by Alexander's four generals (the four wings in Daniel 7:6). Daniel also speaks of a fourth dreadful and most fierce empire, the Roman Empire (Kingdom 4 beginning in 63 B.C.), which had ten caesars (from Julius to Vespasian), some of whom who were contemporaries of Jesus Christ and were ruling when Christ's Kingdom's came during that first century A.D. The Roman Empire was a syncretism of all other kingdoms prior to it, especially that of its predecessor Greece. The Roman emperors aligned themselves against Christ, claiming that there was no other name under heaven whereby men may be saved except through Caesar.[125] In the Roman Empire, worship of Caesar and unconditional obedience to Roman law were considered salvific. Into this world ruled by Satan, the Prince of Darkness, came the light of Jesus Christ, His apostles and His Church. "I am the Light of the World," said Jesus, "He who follows Me shall not walk in darkness, but have the light of life."[126] The world of the first century was filled with emperor worship and idolatrous cult practices,

---

[124] Dan 2:24-45.

[125] Contrary to Acts 4:12.

[126] John 8:12.

which is what St. John was addressing to the seven churches of Asia Minor in the Revelation of Jesus Christ.[127] The first century Jewish nation and the city of Jerusalem, and Rome for that matter, were filled with idolatry, hypocrisy, sickness, disease, and demon possession.

Daniel describes the final portion of the image, its feet and toes, as partly made of iron and partly made of clay. The iron portion of this iron and clay composite represented the Roman Empire previously mentioned, and the portion made of clay represented Jerusalem of the people of God. These two did not mix for they both despised each other. Why is Israel depicted as clay? Again, interpreting Scripture with Scripture—the hermeneutical tool of *analogy of Scripture*. Because the Children of Israel were many times referred to in Scripture throughout redemptive history as the clay of God in the Potter's hand.[128] This would be the final worldly kingdom that was a mix of pagan Rome and apostate Jerusalem, both of whom inspired by the devil, wanted to murder Christ and His Church. It would come to pass during the last of the last days of the House of Israel that pagan Rome, the premier cult of emperor worship, along with the unbelieving and Caesar-worshipping Jerusalem in Judea would ally together against the Lord's people. Rome thought with the destruction of Jerusalem and the temple, it could wipe out the rebellious Jews, whom they hated with passion, as well as the pestiferous and atheistic Christians, whom they hated for their "idolatry" and treason.[129] At this time in the first century, Christians were sorely persecuted for their refusal to worship all of the gods of Rome; they were considered "unbelievers" or "atheists."[130] Recalling that the Gospel of Jesus Christ went first to the Jews and then to the Gentiles, the Church, by the time of the Great Tribulation had adherents from both groups from all over the then-known world, which was the Roman Empire.[131] During the days of this fourth

---

[127] Rev 2-3.

[128] Isa 45:9; 64:8; Jer 18:6.

[129] The Christians acknowledged "another king," namely Jesus Christ, whom they considered above Caesar.

[130] See Josephus' The Wars of the Jews.

[131] Col 1:3-6.

dreadful, iron-toothed beast called the Empire of Rome, the Roman Empire would be split into two components that would not mix: the allied forces of Rome and apostate Jerusalem. These two would wage war against Yahweh God, His Christ, and His holy people between A.D. 66-70.[132] God, however, would turn the hearts of the Romans against Jerusalem, which was the reason for the destruction of the City and its temple. Prior to the fall of Jerusalem, the Church had escaped the doomed city to head toward the mountains as Jesus had exhorted.[133] The end of the Old Covenant Age had come.[134] With the Lord's coming, or Parousia, Jesus Christ established His Kingdom that broke into pieces all other kingdoms. Furthermore, this Kingdom would stand forever.[135]

Redemptive History from Daniel to John the Baptizer

From the days of Daniel (586 B.C.) until the days that John the Baptizer came preaching a baptism of repentance (A.D. 26) saying, "The Kingdom of God is at hand," the prophets of Israel continued speaking and pointing the Jews to the coming Messiah and His Kingdom. Nebuchadnezzar, the great king, moved by the Spirit of God, finally acknowledged that "…His dominion is an everlasting dominion, and His kingdom is from generation to generation."[136] Daniel saw the Christ to come in his visions and referred to Him as the "Ancient of Days." In another vision, Daniel seems to refer to God Himself as the Ancient of Days. Daniel's Christ, as Ancient of Days, strikingly has the same resemblance and heavenly environment as the Son of Man about whom St. John was speaking in the Revelation of Jesus Christ.[137] Daniel sees the Ancient of Days, who in Daniel's day was the preincarnate Word, seated in heaven having received His

---

[132] C.f. Ps(s) 2.

[133] Luke 21:20-21.

[134] Matt 24:34-36.

[135] Dan 12:44-45; 2 Sam 7:12.

[136] Dan 4:34-35.

[137] Dan 7:9-14; Rev 1:12-20.

Kingdom as a reward for his redemptive work on behalf of God's people. Daniel also sees the coming of the Son of Man on the clouds of heaven as the presence of God Himself, coming unto His Father to receive His Kingdom.[138] The Son of Man ascends to God, His Father, to receive His Kingdom, dominion, and glory, that all peoples, nations, and languages should serve Him. Daniel continued: "His dominion is an everlasting dominion, which shall not pass away, and His kingdom the one which shall not be destroyed."

As the Book of Daniel closes in Chapter 12, he tells his people that they would realize a time of trouble before Messiah's coming on the clouds. Their hope, which would anchor their soul, would be rooted and grounded in the prophecy that "...your people shall be delivered, everyone who is found written in the book. And many of those who sleep in the dust of the earth shall awake, some to everlasting life, some to shame and everlasting contempt (abhorrence)." This seems to be a reference both to Christ's Resurrection, wherein He took those righteous dead in Paradise, Abraham's bosom, to heaven during His Ascension, and to the First Resurrection of those righteous dead from among the House of Israel at the coming of the Lord Jesus, His Parousia, in A.D. 70. Now, sharing my current and studied findings on these topics, I tread lightly writing about the resurrections in Sacred Scripture since we have some dogmatic declarations by the Church regarding these topics and some areas still in contemplation, discourse, and theological debate. During Christ's Parousia, which Daniel referred to as the end of the days of Israel, wherein the First Resurrection would take place, the righteous dead since the days of Adam; plus the righteous dead who gave their lives for the testimony of Jesus during the Great Tribulation (A.D. 66-70); and those who were alive, persevering in the faith of Jesus and remaining during the time of Christ's Parousia in A.D. 70, as first fruits of the tribes of Israel and of those saved from among the Gentiles, would be partakers of the First Resurrection.[139] All of these partakers of that First Resurrection would be

---

[138] Dan 7:13; c.f., Matt 24:30; 26:64.

[139] A key to understanding the First Resurrection is seeing that all of the sealed and saved of God since the beginning of time would partake of this First Resurrection and would reign with Christ during His current Thousand-Year reign until all of His enemies are made a footstool for His feet.

those whose names were written in the Book of Life.[140] All of those partaking of the First Resurrection are with the Lord in heaven now, even those who were alive at His Parousia and had subsequently died. The rest of the wicked dead, both from the house of Israel and from among the Gentiles, would not rise during the Parousia, but would be reserved for the Second Death at the Final Judgment of the living and the dead, when Christ returns in our future after His current reign.[141] Sadly, Daniel wanted to understand these words from God, but God would not permit his understanding at that time. Daniel saw the book of the prophecy sealed until the end of the 70 weeks. The prophecy would not be unsealed until the Revelation of Jesus Christ and would be unsealed by Jesus Christ Himself as the Lamb who was found worthy to open the seals and to know and to speak about that which He saw, which was the end of the holy people.[142]

Daniel then sees two men speaking to one another as one asks when these things shall be fulfilled, to which the other responds by referring to the end of the Great Tribulation by saying, "that it shall be for a time, times, and a half of time; and when the power of the holy people has been completely shattered, all these things shall be finished."[143] Staying within the context of the Book of Daniel and that of redemptive history, we can discern that the second man clothed in linen was stating that these things shall come to pass and be finished at the end of the Great Tribulation of A.D. 66-70, when the Holy City and its Old Covenant system would be completely shattered or abrogated. Finally, we see the last reference to the Great Tribulation with regard to its three-and-a-half-year length of time as it begins with the Jews taking away of the daily sacrifices on behalf of the emperor (A.D. 67) through to the time the Jerusalem temple was made desolate. This period between these two events is spoken of as 1,290 days.[144] The blessing would come to those who would persevere in the faith until the end of that period in A.D. 70. The First Resurrection would be the reward

---

[140] Dan 7:10; 12:1, 4; Rev 3:5; 13:8; 17:8; 20:12, 15; 21:27; 22:19.

[141] Dan 12:1-3, 7; Rev 2:11; 20:4-6, 14; 21:8.

[142] Rev 5.

[143] Dan 12:7.

[144] Dan 12:11-13.

and blessing to those who survived in the faith beyond the destruction of the city, which is spoken of as being 1,335 days.[145] Daniel is then comforted that he will arise to his inheritance at the end of the days of Covenant Israel.

In the Old Testament, beyond the prophet Daniel, the house of Israel had its hope and joy anchored in the words of the prophets who spoke of the Mountain of the Lord's House being exalted above all mountains and filling the earth. This is a prophetic reference to the Kingdom of God being above all other kingdoms of the earth and as one that would fill the entire earth with the Law (Word) of God. This should bring encouragement to every living Christian that Christ's Kingdom is invincible and destined to worldwide victory before Christ returns to judge the living and the dead. The term, "Mountain of the Lord's House," is a name for the presence of Yahweh God among His covenant people in the Holy Convocation, the Assembly, the Church, the New Jerusalem. The elect or chosen people of the house of Israel rejoiced in the Kingdom of God's filling the earth. Recall that this Mountain of the Lord's House is none other than the stone cut out without hands from the image in Nebuchadnezzar's dream. This stone struck the entire image in a devastating blow representing the Kingdom of God's confronting and crushing the power of Rome and apostate Jerusalem. While interpreting the dream, Daniel said that this stone became a great mountain and filled the whole earth. Mountains have always been a prophetic picture of kingdoms, and God is atop this, His holy mountain, which consists of all His people and all of the creation that He created. Furthermore, this mountain, as Daniel has spoken, has already crushed all previous kingdoms and is now filling the earth even to this day.[146] The Psalmists proclaim the Kingdom of God, the Mountain of Yahweh's House,[147] as a place reserved for those who love Yahweh God and who cleanse themselves from sin while obeying Him,[148] as it is written: "Who may ascend the mountain of the Lord? Who may stand in his holy place?

---

[145] Matt 24:13.

[146] Dan 2:35, 45; Rev 21:26.

[147] In the Old Testament, the name of God, "Yahweh," is translated, "LORD," based on the tradition that the Hebrews did not say the name, "Yahweh," out of respect for the name of God. The Mountain of the LORD's House, could rightly be translated, "The Mountain of Yahweh's House."

[148] Rev 21:27.

The one who has clean hands and a pure heart, who does not trust in an idol or swear by a false god. They will receive blessing from the Lord and vindication from God their Savior. Such is the generation of those who seek him, who seek your face, God of Jacob."[149] God's City is the New Jerusalem, Zion, a temple made without hands,[150] the Kingdom of God, and indeed the Church of Jesus Christ. It seems, though, that the scope and sovereignty of the Kingdom of God is also greater than the Church since the Most High rules over all. Jesus Christ is Lord, and "great is the Lord, and most worthy of praise, in the city of our God, his holy mountain. Beautiful in its loftiness, the joy of the whole earth, like the heights of Zaphon is Mount Zion, the city of the Great King. God is in her citadels; he has shown himself to be her fortress."[151]

Finally, the prophets Micah and Isaiah, building upon our understanding of the words of Daniel about the growing Kingdom, present the clearest view of the growth of the Kingdom of God in the latter days, or last days of Old Covenant Israel.[152] In summary, the Lord Himself establishes the Kingdom of God in the Last Days beginning with the ministry of Jesus Christ and continuing with His sacrifice on the cross, His resurrection, His obtaining His Lordship, and His coming on the clouds of glory with the holy angels and saints in judgment upon Israel in A.D. 70. Furthermore, with the abrogation of the earthly and faithless Jerusalem, its temple, its priesthood, and its redemptive sacrifices at the coming of the Lord at the end of the Great Tribulation of those latter days, the Kingdom of God came with great power and has since been filling the entire earth. This is the fulfillment of Daniel's vision of the stone that destroyed all other kingdoms. Today, the Church and the Kingdom of God that empowers her, is still growing and will continue to do so until all of Christ's enemies are under His feet. The world still needs to declare an unconditional surrender to the King and His Laws.

The Church, through the preaching of the Word of God and its service of the Sacraments, disciples the nations for obedience to the faith, to bring healing

---

[149] Ps(s) 24.

[150] Rev 21:22-27.

[151] Ps(s) 48:1-3.

[152] Mic. 4:1-8; Isa 2:1-5.

to the nations. The Church as well as Wisdom herself calls daily to all nations: "Come hear the Word of the Lord and be healed." The people of God, His kings and priests in Christ, abound in fervent love toward God and toward others. They are desirous of doing good works to all, and praying for all continually. As a result, unregenerate mankind sees these works and looks to God and worships Him as they should. The hope in the heart of the covenant believer in Christ, the true Jew, is that, as the Word of the Lord goes forth from the Lord's House, Zion, men will embrace the Commandments of God, the Law of God, from the heart and obey that word to the extent that individuals, families, tribes, and nations will love the Lord their God with all of their heart, and then love their neighbors as themselves. As a result, they will experience blessings of private property and fruitful lands, as well as the transformation of their weapons of warfare into implements of production, thus ushering in progressive blessings all over the earth of righteousness, peace, and joy in the Holy Spirit. As mentioned earlier, here is that message, spoken by Micah and Isaiah regarding the Kingdom of God that is filling the earth and saving the nations. This is not a picture of heaven, but a picture of God's Kingdom having come and continuing to come *on earth*, and this all happening before the Final Judgment of God and the return of Christ Jesus to judge the living and the dead at the end of time, referred to as the Second Coming. The beautiful prophecy from Micah was delivered to God's people nearly 700 years before Messiah was born:

> *Micah 4: In the last days the mountain of the Lord's temple will be established as the highest of the mountains; it will be exalted above the hills, and peoples will stream to it. 2 Many nations will come and say, "Come, let us go up to the mountain of the Lord, to the temple of the God of Jacob. He will teach us his ways, so that we may walk in his paths." The law will go out from Zion, the word of the Lord from Jerusalem. 3 He will judge between many peoples and will settle disputes for strong nations far and wide. They will beat their swords into plowshares and their spears into pruning hooks. Nation will not take up sword against nation, nor will they train for war anymore. 4 Everyone will sit under their own vine and under their own fig tree, and no one will make them afraid,*

for the Lord Almighty has spoken. 5 All the nations may walk in the name of their gods, but we will walk in the name of the Lord our God for ever and ever. 6 "In that day," declares the Lord, "I will gather the lame; I will assemble the exiles and those I have brought to grief. 7 I will make the lame my remnant, those driven away a strong nation. The Lord will rule over them in Mount Zion from that day and forever. 8 As for you, watchtower of the flock, stronghold of Daughter Zion, the former dominion will be restored to you; kingship will come to Daughter Jerusalem."

TABLE 4. JESUS PREPARED HIS DISCIPLES FOR THE LAST DAYS OF THE FIRST COVENANT AND FOR THE INAUGURATION OF THE KINGDOM OF GOD

Table 4, Chronological Timeline 5, begins with Jesus Christ's ministry in A.D. 26, and ends with Christ's Parousia culminating in the destruction of Jerusalem and its temple in A.D. 70, representing a time span of 43 ½ years. We will address here all of the events associated with

Christ's Parousia, which includes the Kingdom of God having come in power,[153] the binding of Satan,[154] the First Resurrection,[155] and the inauguration of the Thousand-Year Reign of Christ[156] (an event which was synonymous with the inauguration of the New Heavens and New Earth).[157] It seems that from Sacred Scripture, one can deduce that all of these events, among many others, occurred as it was written in the prophets, the Gospels, the New Testament epistles, and the Revelation of Jesus Christ. That appearing, or coming of Christ, as Daniel prophesied, was the appointed time for the sorely persecuted and martyred saints of the first century and beyond to possess the Kingdom, the New Jerusalem having come from above, the Mother of us all.[158]

---

[153] Matt 24:30; Mark 9:1; and c.f., Rev 22:20.

[154] Rev 20:1-3, 7-10.

[155] Rev 20:4-6.

[156] Rev 20:4-5, a symbolic Thousand-Year duration that meant a reign lasting as long as determined by God, vs. a literal one thousand years, as will be shown.

[157] 2 Pet 3:13; Rev 21.

[158] Dan 7:21-22; Rev 21.

Table 4. Jesus Prepared His Disciples for the Last Days of the First Covenant and for His Coming

The Last Days of Israel, the City and Temple of Jerusalem, and the First Covenant

Chronological Timeline	A.D. 30 – A.D. 70 The Old Testament Kingdom and the New Test Kingdom OVERLAP.		The Last Hour 1 John 2:18

The Great Tribulation

A.D. 26	A.D. 30		A.D. 66	A.D. 70

A.D. 26

Jesus the Christ

Comes preaching and teaching about the Gospel of Kingdom, with healing signs and wonders bearing witness.

A.D. 30

Jesus' Ascension

Jesus receives His Kingdom. Holy Spirit is poured out as a sign of the Last Days of Israel.

Jesus' Church

Preaches the Gospel of the Kingdom in all the world (the Roman empire) prior to and during the Great Tribulation. Col 1:6.

A.D. 66

A.D. 70

The Great Tribulation

The Great Distress, the test upon the entire World, the Roman Empire of the first century. The greatest tribulation that had ever been, or ever would be. Lasted 3 ½ years; also known as a time, times, and a half of time; 1290 days; and 42 months. Caesar Nero, whose name in Hebrew equaled 666, led the greatest persecution of Christians ever, which culminated in the loss of the Jewish nation and its whole world (the city and its temple). See Josephus, War of the Jews. See Ecclesiastical History, Eusebius. See St Benedict XVI, Jesus of Nazareth.

The Revelation of Jesus Christ given By God to Jesus and then to St. John around A.D. 66; was preached to the 7 Churches of Asia Minor. Jesus opened the seal and the time of His coming in salvation and judgment was revealed to Him.

Notable Messages from Jesus about His Immanent Appearing and the Coming of His Kingdom in A.D. 70.

- His purpose was to preach the Kingdom, and all nations would flow into it
- His Kingdom to be sought first and God would grant all that was needed
- His Kingdom would grow like a mustard seed and fill the earth
- He was the King of the Kingdom
- Warned the rulers, scribes, Pharisees that the Kingdom would be taken from them and given to a nation bearing the fruits of it
- Warned Jerusalem and its temple would be left desolate
- The Kingdom of God would be preached in all the world and then the end would come (end of the Kingdom of Israel/Jerusalem/symbolically as Babylon)
- Warned the generation He was speaking to would see the end of the city, the Great Tribulation, and the end of the temple
- He comes for salvation and judgment with ten thousands of His saints and angels
- Spoke of His coming, His appearing, the sign of the Son of Man in heaven
- Spoke of the horrors of the coming Great Tribulation during the generation living and told the disciples to persevere and watch
- Said there are some hearing His words who would not taste death until they saw the Kingdom of God coming, or present with power
- Apostles would not have gone throughout all the cities of Israel BEFORE the Son of Man comes
- Insinuated that John the Apostle may be alive when He returns
- Proclaimed His current Kingship and Lordship by saying all authority in heaven and earth was His.
- Christ commanded that they, therefore, make disciples of the nations, teaching them to obey all that He taught them.

From the 1st Century Christian's View

The Figurative 1000-Year Reign of Christ; also known as the Inaugurated New Heavens and New Earth; and the Growth of the Holy Mountain, Zion, the New Jerusalem, the Church.

Christ's current reign continues until all His enemies are made a footstool for His feet. Ps(s) 110, Rev 20, 21, and 22 The continuing fulfillment of Isa 2, Mic 4.

The coming of the Lord, also known as Christ's appearing, Christ's Parousia, Christ's coming on the clouds having occurred on the 1st of Tishri, A.D. 70.

The Great Day of the Lord

Christ's Coming in Judgment upon unbelieving Israel

End of Old Testament Jerusalem, its temple, sacrifices, and priesthood

Sign of the Son of Man in Heaven

First Resurrection of the first century martyrs

Judgment made in favor of the saints

Christ's Judgment upon Rome, the beginning of its end

Shaking of the Old Heavens and Old Earth (Heb 12)

Great feast of the birds of the dead on the battlefield outside of Jerusalem

Inaugurated New Heavens and New Earth (Rev 21)

The Lamb's Bride had made herself ready for the Marriage Supper of the Lamb

Christ's salvation of His Church

Times of refreshing from the Lord

The binding of Satan and his placement in the abyss to no longer deceive the nations against Christ

Rev 19:6 "Hallelujah! For the Lord our God the Almighty reigns. 7 Let us rejoice and exult and give him the glory, for the marriage of the Lamb has come, and his Bride has made herself ready.

"I Must Preach the Kingdom of God...Because for This Purpose I Have Been Sent"

Jesus Christ's ministry began with His preaching the good news of the Kingdom of God being present in Himself as well as its coming being at hand, or near.[159] "I must preach the Kingdom of God to the other cities also, because for this purpose I have been sent."[160] He also taught his disciples to preach the same.[161] The message of the Lord's reign was a joyful noise in the ears of those who longed for the redemption of Israel, the restoration of the Kingdom of God to the people of God, Israel. The people who loved Yahweh God and Messiah's and His Kingdom's coming looked forward to the end of the age and the coming of the Messiah King. The Book of the Acts of the Apostles provides clear evidence that St. Philip, St. Paul, and others preached the Gospel of the Kingdom of God.[162] Christ's purpose was to preach the Kingdom to the Jews first so that they and their rulers could escape the coming wrath of God that targeted the disobedient within the city of Jerusalem, its rulers, and its people.[163] The corrupt rulers of Jerusalem during the days of Jesus' ministry had descended from those Jews throughout history who murdered their own prophets and sought to murder Christ Jesus, also. During Jesus' trial for blasphemy and insurrection, the people screamed for a murderer, Barabbas, to be spared while rejecting Jesus Christ, their Messiah Prince before Pontius Pilate. The final horrifying and ignorant cry of the apostates was for Christ's blood to be upon them and their children.[164] (Note: Jesus prayed while upon the cross, "Father, forgive them, for they know not what they do"). After Jesus' Death, Resurrection, and Ascension to heaven, His apostles and disciples continued to call the Jews and the Gentiles to repentance for the next 40 years until the city of Jerusalem was destroyed. Josephus

---

[159] Matt 12:28; Mark 1:15.

[160] Luke 4:43.

[161] Matt 10:7, 24:14.

[162] Acts 8:12; 17:7; 20:25; 28:31.

[163] Matt 3:5-12.

[164] Matt 27:25.

records that by the time of the Great Tribulation during the Jewish war, the apostasy of the rulers and people of Jerusalem who had rejected Christ Jesus was irreparable. "If the Romans hadn't destroyed these villains, the earth would have swallowed them up like Sodom, for the generation which was in it was far more ungodly than the men on whom these punishments had in former times fallen. By their madness, the whole nation came to be ruined."[165] On this topic, Schaff adds, "Thus, therefore, must one of the best Roman Emperors [Vespasian] execute the long threatened judgment of God and the most learned Jew of his time describe it [Josephus], and thereby, without willing or knowing it, bear testimony of the truth of the prophecy and the divinity of the mission of Jesus Christ, the rejection of whom brought all this and the subsequent misfortune upon the apostate race."[166]

Jesus' instruction regarding the Kingdom of God was multifaceted. He taught that His disciples should not fret about having their needs met in this world, but that they were to seek first the Kingdom of God, then all other things needed or desired would be granted them by God as a result. This instruction would prove critically valuable during the Great Tribulation that was coming upon these first century saints. Jesus taught that His Kingdom would grow incrementally like a mustard seed and fill the earth according to the prophecies of Daniel, Isaiah, and Micah, about which we've spoken above. Jesus in no uncertain terms declared that He was the King of the Kingdom of God present, and that there was yet to be a Kingdom to come and that in power. He clearly warned the Jews that their city of Jerusalem and its temple would be left desolate because her inhabitants had left the faith of Abraham and Moses and would neither hear Jesus' words, nor find salvation in His name, who told them His burden would be light and from whom would come rest for their souls. Yet Jesus' message was destined beyond Jerusalem, for He said that the Kingdom of God would be preached in all the world (the then-known world) which was the entire Roman Empire, and then the end (the end of the first covenant age) would come. He was speaking specifically of the end of the Kingdom of Israel, Old

---

[165] Flavius Josephus - <u>The Wars of the Jews</u>, p. 292, or in some multivolume sets, Book V. 13, 6.

[166] Schaff, The Great Tribulation, <u>The History of the Christian Church</u>, Volume 1, <u>The Wars of the Jews</u>, p. 399.

Testament Jerusalem, the intended Bride of God, who instead of becoming the priestly daughter nation of Yahweh God, became "Babylon the Great" (the city of captivity to sin and error), the Mother of Harlots and of the Abominations of the Earth.[167] The priestly daughter city of Jerusalem, who "played the whore with pagan Rome" and other nations, abandoned her faithfulness to God and received her just punishment by fire.[168] Jesus warned His Jewish followers and his general audiences that they must be saved from that perverted generation of sinners and unbelievers who always looked for a sign beyond Christ Jesus Himself.[169] St. Peter and St. Paul also warned the Christians from among the Jews and the Gentiles respectively that the generation then living, hearing their words, were the terminal generation who would see the end of Old Covenant Jerusalem and its temple. They exhorted those inside and outside of the Jewish synagogues that they must come out and be separate from that perverse, wicked, and adulterous generation.[170] That terminal generation of the first century was warned that they would see the end of the city, would endure the Great Tribulation, and would see the desolation of the Jerusalem temple, which would be dissolved by fire, as elements melting with fervent heat.[171] This is why St. Peter told the dispersed Jews to embrace holy conduct and godliness prior to the appearing of their Lord in great power, all having occurred in A.D. 70.[172]

Jesus prophesied that He would soon come for salvation and judgment with at least ten thousand of His saints and angels. This event would be His coming, also referred to in Scripture as His appearing, His Parousia, and the sign of the Son of Man in Heaven.[173] He also warned His followers of the horrors of the coming Great Tribulation and exhorted them to persevere and watch, stay awake

---

[167] Rev 17:5.

[168] Lev 21:9; 2 Pet 3:10-12.

[169] Matt 12:39, 45; 16:4; 17:17; 23:36; 24:34.

[170] Acts 2:40; Phil. 2:15.

[171] 2 Pet 3:12-13.

[172] 2 Pet 3:11; 1 Thess 4:13—5:6.

[173] Matt 24:30-31.

and pursue holiness unto the end to be saved.[174] Jesus exhorted His disciples not to love their lives even unto death, as a precursor to St. Paul's message that with much tribulation one would enter the Kingdom of God.[175] Christ also promised His disciples and followers that any who had left everything—houses, lands, fathers, mothers, children—and would become detached from all things for the sake of following Christ and His Kingdom would receive in return all that was given up, a hundredfold return, but with persecutions.[176] Those forsaking all to follow Christ and who would not be ashamed of His name would, in the end, receive eternal life.[177]

Jesus made a quite peculiar statement to His disciples, as recorded in all three synoptic Gospels, that there were some among His apostles who were standing there hearing His words who would not taste death until they saw the Kingdom of God coming in power.[178] These were striking verses of truth from which we learned that some of those disciples saw the coming of the Lord in power, Christ's Parousia, in the first century. We know that the Apostle John was alive at our Lord's Coming in power in A.D. 70 because prior to the destruction of Jerusalem and its temple, John was given the Revelation of Jesus Christ from Jesus Himself, who had received it from His Father. And St. John continued to live after the year of the conflagration of Jerusalem and, according to St. Irenaeus, was seen nearly up to the second century.[179] St. John wrote the Revelation of Jesus Christ as he saw the vision from the Isle of Patmos around A.D. 65 or 66, prior to the three-and-a-half years of Great Tribulation that began in A.D. 66. The multiple visions within John's Revelation of Jesus Christ clearly spoke in symbolic and apocalyptic terms of the destruction of the city, its temple, and the coming of Christ in salvation for His elect people as well as the judgment of the apostate Jews and their rulers.

---

[174] Matt 10:22; 24:13.

[175] Acts 14:21-22.

[176] Matt 19:29.

[177] Mark 10:30.

[178] Matt 16:28; Mark 9:1; Luke 9:27.

[179] Against Heresies, 5.30.3.

John's Revelation of Jesus Christ was a book of immediate relevance and great comfort to the seven churches to whom it was written. It requires an interpretation based on the historical context, the language of the time, and the relevance it had to its first century audience. The interpretation without doubt had to have been relevant to its first century audience of Asia Minor, where the seven churches existed to whom the prophecy was addressed.

The first century interpretation notwithstanding, there are many principles that today's Church can embrace from the first-century understanding of the entire book. Another key to the first century relevance of the Revelation is the date in which the Revelation was seen and written. A popular majority of today's theologians state that the Revelation was written during the reign of Emperor Domitian; however, St. Irenaeus, upon whom most of these theologians rely, did not say in his writings definitively and without dispute that the Revelation of Jesus Christ was seen in the days of Domitian but given his use of the language at the time could have said that St. John *himself* was alive and was seen in the days of Domitian. The ancient Greek language could easily support both interpretations. This would correspond to Jesus' words about some of the disciples not tasting death until the Kingdom came in power.[180] This author holds to the "early" dating of Revelation, which would align first century events with their symbolic portrayals in the book. Irenaeus said, "For it/he was seen, not long ago, but almost in our generation, near the end of Domitian's reign." A dating of the Revelation of Jesus Christ after A.D.70, does not correlate with the historical events of the time after the fall of Jerusalem, nor the manifold internal evidence to the contrary in the Revelation of Jesus Christ itself.[181] The early dating of the Revelation is important for the sake of understanding the warning of this prophecy as it corresponds to God's Days of Vengeance upon apostate Israel and the empowering of the New Jerusalem, the Church of Jesus Christ, which would then be saved from her enemies and begin to spread her message of healing throughout the entire world from A.D. 70, forward.

---

[180] See David Chilton's, Days of Vengeance, on the dating of the Revelation.

[181] An excellent analysis of the Revelation's author and date of origin can be found in David Chilton's Days of Vengeance, pp. 1-6. Chilton quotes from St. Irenaeus and Eusebius' Ecclesiastical History regarding the dating of the Revelation.

Interestingly, Jesus told His apostles that they would not have gone thru all the cities of Israel preaching, teaching, and healing BEFORE the Son of Man comes or returns.[182] This statement of Jesus, along with the very interesting banter among the apostles that the Apostle John would still be alive when Jesus returned gives crystal clear evidence that the Lord Jesus intended to return, as He did in A.D. 70, to destroy the shakable, temporary Old Covenant system with its types and shadows, bring vengeance upon the sinners and persecutors of His Church, bring salvation to His elect people who persevered through the Great Tribulation, and inaugurate the Kingdom of God's coming along with that of the New Heavens and New Earth.[183] The Revelation itself uses phrases, such as "I come quickly," "the time is at hand," and "soon," none of which could possibly mean hundreds and thousands of years from the time the words were uttered.

Finally, prior to Jesus' departing from His disciples for His throne in heaven, He spoke to them, saying, "All authority has been given to Me in heaven and on earth. Go, therefore and make disciples of all the nations, baptizing them in the name of the Father and of the Son and of the Holy Spirit, teaching them to observe all things that I have commanded you; and lo, I am with you always, even to the end of the age."[184] Here Jesus affirms that the nations were to be instructed in the Commandments of God and to live in holiness accordingly. He comforted His disciples by adding that He would be with them even to the end of the age, which was the remaining 40 years of the Old Covenant age. Furthermore, He and His Father sent forth the Spirit of God, the Comforter, to lead and guide His people into all truth. It should be noted that Jesus still has all authority, is still seated as King and Ruler of the universe, and is still with us today even unto the end of this age of the Kingdom. These last words of Jesus were of critical importance to His people and would have been a great comfort to those disciples in the first century, helping them to persevere through the persecution, tribulation, and martyrdom to come for His name's sake. Christ's Ascension to heaven and all its significance has been celebrated as the Feast of

---

[182] Matt 10:23.

[183] John 21:20-23.

[184] Matt 28:18-20.

the Ascension of Jesus Christ (also called the Solemnity of the Ascension of Jesus Christ) and is still celebrated today as one of the ecumenical feasts of Christian churches, ranking with the feasts of the Passion and Pentecost.

Jesus' Coming with His Kingdom Was Immanent to the First Century Church

A Hebrew Christian would have understood the Revelation of Jesus Christ as given by St. John as the final warning to Christians to depart from Jerusalem, Babylon the Great, before it would be leveled to the ground in the conflagration of A.D. 70.[185] Apart from a first century understanding of the Lord's coming and the destruction of Jerusalem, the Revelation of Jesus Christ with its message that Christ was "coming quickly" would make little useful sense to its first century audience. The description of the cities, the line-up of Roman emperors, the Churches of Asia Minor, the beasts symbolizing Rome and apostate Jerusalem, the armies and the battle of Mount Megiddo, have in this author's opinion little to no other alignment with real places, events, or things apart from the first century.[186] Added to this first century relevance, the Revelation presents to every succeeding generation since the first century the New Jerusalem and the New

---

[185] Church Historian Eusebius records in his Ecclesiastical Histories: "The whole body, however, of the church at Jerusalem, having been commanded by a divine revelation, given to men of approved piety there before the war, removed from the city, and dwelt at a certain town beyond the Jordan, called Pella. Here, those that believed in Christ, having removed from Jerusalem, as if holy men had entirely abandoned the royal city itself, and the whole land of Judea: the divine justice, for their crimes against Christ and his apostles, finally overtook them, totally destroying the whole generation of these evildoers from the earth." Hist., Book III, Chapter V, page 86. For Eusebius' entire expose of the events prior to, during, and after the Great Tribulation of the first century, read all of Book III, Chapters XIX-XXIX.

[186] As an example of the alignment of the Revelation of Jesus Christ with first century reality, the term Armageddon is a symbolic location combining the term "mountain," or "har," in Hebrew with the real location in the Middle East of the Valley of Megiddo. There is no literal "Mount Megiddo;" therefore, the term Mount Megiddo, or Armageddon, is a symbolic reference to the place where the Lord Jesus and His armies confronted apostate Jerusalem. Compare this to Elijah's confrontation with Baal on Mount Carmel as recorded in 1 Kings 18..

Heavens and Earth, both of which began at Christ's Parousia and continue to bring forth blessing and healing in all of the earth in these days of the current reign of Jesus.

Why are some reluctant to speak these truths including the truth that the Lord remains in the heavens until all His enemies are made a footstool for His feet? Some fear that if, as the Scriptures truly teach, Jesus Christ remains in the heavens seated as King until the vanquishing of His enemies, then we are making it easy for people to sin. They will not fear an immanent Second Coming and thus remain in their debauchery versus sanctifying themselves and their lives unto holiness. Furthermore, many who would hear this teaching of our Lord's having come in A.D. 70 may accuse us of denying or delaying His Second Coming sort of like St. James accusing some members of *his* Jewish audience of saying, "where is the promise of His coming?" Suffice it to say, Jesus Christ did indeed come in the clouds in A.D. 70 as He promised. To speak the truth that Christ continues reigning over all from His throne in heaven until all enemies are defeated is not saying that He is "delaying" nor is it "denying His coming." His coming, or His Parousia, did happen when it was supposed to happen in the first century. There was no inadvertent delay. Furthermore, as the Church has dogmatically decreed, He will come again to judge the living and the dead when all His enemies are under His feet—Christ's Second Coming as it has been dogmatically defined in the Church's creeds. Another significant point to be made is that He said to St. John that He was coming soon and that His reward was with Him, and "soon," meant in every respect to the languages into which this word has been translated as "soon." It literally meant nothing other than "immanently." These words, "soon," "quickly," or "at hand," are not the result of Christ not knowing the meaning of the words He chose and are not words that one can freely allegorize to deny His coming with His Kingdom in A.D. 70. The word "soon" has never in its grammatical history meant hundreds or thousands of years into the future, an interpretation which would render Revelation's warning meaningless to those Christians who originally heard the message in the first century, and needed to know He was coming "soon." In fact, Jesus said that if those days of the first century Great Tribulation were not cut short, no one would have been saved; yet, for the elect's sake, the days until His coming in the first century were cut short.[187] So, the eschatological and Kingdom conclusions within this book concerning John's Revelation of Jesus Christ do not in any way besmirch God's promises. They simply hold that they were fulfilled in the first century. Yet, given that truth, this book never contradicts or denies a future return of Christ at the expiration of His current Thousand-Year Reign. One should not, however, manipulate the Church with inaccurate eschatological interpretations of Scripture to shape or misshape people's behavior. It is best to speak the truth that our Lord may not return for hundreds if not thousands of years; therefore, one should be holy, mature spiritually and in every other way, get busy, and start building treasure in heaven while Christianizing every realm of life on earth: one's self, then one's family, and then everything beyond those realms as God gives grace. We are to abound in love and press God's love into every realm of life, lest we become idle and unfruitful in the knowledge of God and Christ.

Church historian Eusebius (A.D. 260-A.D. 340), Jewish General Josephus (b. A.D. 37), 20th century church historian Philip Schaff, the late Pope Benedict XVI (in his book Jesus of Nazareth), and authors like the late David Chilton and many others understood the critical significance of Jesus' prophetic words concerning Jerusalem as being fulfilled during the first century. One could ask, "Why didn't the Greek Church fathers, known also as the Ante Nicene fathers, who wrote after the first century, speak about the destruction of Jerusalem as being the end of the age?" One answer is that the Ante-Nicene Fathers, being Greek, primarily interpreted Scripture as they did all literature, using an allegorical hermeneutical method as opposed to a historical-grammatical method, where the symbolic and literal interpretation is applied as necessary given the language and the historical milieu.[188] The Revelation of Jesus Christ is "the most biblical book in the Bible," as one philosopher and theologian spoke, meaning that if one were not to understand the Old Testament, one could not hope to understand the language, symbolism, and warnings of the Revelation.[189] We can say, however, that the early Church fathers, such as St. Athanasius (4th century),

---

[187] Matt 24:22.

[188] The position of Dr. R. J. Rushdoony obtained via a phone interview by this author regarding biblical hermeneutics associated with the Ante Nicene Fathers.

[189] Dr. Greg Bahnsen, Commentary on the Revelation of Jesus Christ, Taped lecture series.

understood the coming of the Kingdom and its growing nature throughout the entire earth as having taken place during the first century and continuing on afterwards. Athanasius the Great, a fourth century Patriarch of Alexandria wrote, "When the sun has come, darkness prevails no longer; any of it that may be left anywhere is driven away. So also, now that the Divine epiphany of the Word of God has taken place, the darkness of idols prevails no more, and all parts of the world in every direction are enlightened by His teaching."[190] We can, however, thank God that more and more theologians are recognizing the active and very real nature of the rule of Christ in the earth today along with its positive effects in every realm of authority, including the individual's soul, family, Church, and State.

Jesus Christ Destroyed Satan's Deceptive Shroud of Lies, and Is Reclaiming the Earth for God

The Church is young and has been growing in virtue and spiritual graces since the days of Jesus Christ. Actually, the faithful of the children of Israel of the first covenant who were awaiting the Christ to come is the root of this Christian tree that is forever steady in Christ Jesus.[191] Although the Kingdom of God has come in Christ and Christ's reign has been inaugurated and has been progressing for two thousand years, the building and the sanctification of the Church and the Christianizing of the world happens over time and requires work and patience. There is much to do and much to build, and we can be thankful that we are not where we started back in the first century. That is why we all see imperfections and evil around us in every realm of authority. But because of this, many faint and hope that Jesus will return soon and culminate the Kingdom of God, perhaps saving them out of this "evil" world. Yet, God has once and for all through Christ vanquished the power of evil. Sacred Scripture presents the truth that, Jesus came to destroy the deceiving power and horrific works of the devil. This led to his being bound by Christ during His first century Parousia so that Christ's Church

---

[190] Athanasius, <u>On the Incarnation</u>, 55.

[191] Rom 11:17-18.

and the power and presence of Christ's Kingdom could fill the earth and bring all things under His feet. Then He eventually could and would return to judge the living and the dead. Four thousand years passed from the Garden's promise of a Seed to come until Christ Jesus came to earth. Why should we then expect the sinful mess to be cleaned entirely within only two thousand years?

This book is written to adjust such thinking and to renew the mind from defeat and worldwide entropy to a mind that sees Christ's victory being worked out in the earth today. This author is calling for a rational and biblical optimism as well as faith in the power and magnitude of God's grace through Christ. Failing to see the Lordship of Christ over the nations and His victorious building of His Church and His Kingdom in the world exaggerates Satan's powers. This leads to irrational, pessimistic, defeatist life attitudes and cynicism, faithlessness, and depressing hopelessness. It is the Scriptures of the Old and New Testament that gives us warrant and foundation for this renewal of the mind.[192]

Looking back in redemptive history, Jesus warned the rulers, scribes, and Pharisees during His earthly ministry that the Kingdom of God would be taken from them, the first covenant nation of Israel, and given to a nation that would bear the fruits of it. During Christ's preaching, we see that Satan's power was exercised at its height at the point when Jesus was betrayed into the hands of the apostate rulers by a demon-possessed disciple, Judas.[193] Jesus said, "Have you come out, as against a robber, with swords and clubs? When I was with you daily in the temple, you did not try to seize Me. But this is your hour, and the power of darkness."[194]

Today, Jesus Christ is Lord. By virtue of His obedience to God, even to the extent of His submitting to the ignoble death on the cross, He was justified by God His Father through His Resurrection from the dead. He was granted an everlasting kingdom and was exalted to the position of King of Kings and Lord of Lords with all authority and power in the earth. This also means that Jesus

---

[192] C.f., Rom 12:1-2.

[193] Acts 3:12-18.

[194] Luke 22:52-53.

Christ is greater in authority and power than all the angels, including Satan, the adversary of God and mankind. By virtue of His redemptive work at Calvary, Jesus Christ has not only vanquished the power of Satan, who usurped mankind's vicegerency of God in the earth, but He continues to engage in what some have rightly called a cultural "mop-up action" on earth. He, His Church, and His Kingdom clean and rid the earth of the effects of original sin, the devil, and the resulting culture of death that that sin has caused since the Garden of Eden and continues to cause through unbelief and disobedience to God's Word. Jesus Christ came to destroy the works of the devil and did. Jesus bound him, cast him into the abyss while He reigns as Lord of Lords and King of Kings during His Thousand-Year Reign in which we are now living.

Christ's continuing work as High Priest in heaven has made provision for the healing of the nations through the Sacraments of His Church, for by His stripes (His beatings associated with His trial and Crucifixion), we were healed.[195] Jesus of Nazareth went about doing good and healing all who were oppressed by the devil for God was with Him. The Gospels record that Jesus was the all-powerful Light of the world, who, endowed with the Spirit of God, overcame Satan himself in the desert temptations, and then proceeded to cast out the devils that were deceiving, spiritually blinding, making sick and diseased, possessing, and killing God's covenant people, especially those in and around the great city of Jerusalem. His disciples and followers recognized the power in His name, "Jesus," meaning "Yahweh Saves," to command devils to go or to come out. Jesus and His disciples spoke boldly and confidently with hearts of faith in and through His name so that the devils obeyed their commands. Throughout redemptive history, Christians have always confronted the lies of the devil with the truth of God's Word, and the devils, already defeated due to the work of the King on the cross, flee impotently away. Jesus' teaching His disciples with all wisdom and authority, added that the tough cases of demon possession would be resolved through prayer and fasting, a truth that the Church's exorcists have verified for two millennia. Jesus' power was made manifest by His omnipotence to cast out devils with a word, and He showed forth His intentions to save the nations by casting out the devils called "Legion" in the Gentile realm of Gadara and telling the demons to go into a herd

---

[195] Isa 53:5; 1 Pet. 2:24.

of swine, which caused the herd's death. Jesus was cleansing both Jerusalem of the Jews and the Gentile nations of the devil's deception.

During Jesus' earthly ministry, he delegated His authority to the ministry of 70 of His disciples during their formation telling them to heal the sick and say to them, "The Kingdom of God has come near to you."[196] To those folks who would reject the good news of the Kingdom of God, they were to be told by the disciples, "The very dust of your city which clings to us we wipe off against you. Nevertheless, know this, the Kingdom of God has come near you." Jesus mentioned that judgment upon the unbelieving Jews would be more severe for those rejecting the message from His apostles than for those who lived in Sodom before its destruction from heaven. To the wonderment of His disciples upon their returning from their preaching, teaching, and healing ministries recorded in Luke, they stated to their Lord that even the devils themselves were subject to them. Jesus replied to them that He "saw Satan fall like lightning from heaven." He gave them authority to trample on serpents and scorpions, and over all the power of the enemy, such that nothing would hurt them. Nevertheless, He told them not to rejoice in this, that the spirits were subject to them, but rather to rejoice because their names were written in heaven. At that point, Jesus saw the devil being vanquished and cast out of heaven by God. Prior to His departure to heaven for the last time ten days after his Resurrection, Jesus told his disciples that casting out devils would be among the signs that follow their ministry.[197] Jesus also warned His disciples to check their hearts and to remember that only those who do the will of His Father would enter the Kingdom of Heaven, and not simply those who cast out demons in His name, but who do God's will.[198]

After Jesus' Ascension to heaven to sit upon His throne from a vantage point of the Victor's repose, the Church continued to preach, teach, heal, and cast out devils. Jesus and His apostles had wiped the City of Jerusalem clean of devils by A.D. 30. With the addition of St. Paul and his fellow companions and disciples, the God-fearing Gentiles were being converted by the Spirit of God and being

---

[196] Luke 10:1-12, 17-20, 23-24.

[197] Mark 16:16-18.

[198] Matt 7: 21-23.

added to the Church, many of whom were healed of demon possession, diseases, and pagan superstitions. Sadly, as Jesus had taught, the devils that were cast out of Jerusalem and its inhabitants had come back with a vengeance to infest the city and to lead it to its desolation.[199]

The cultural resistance to the truth of the Kingdom of God is due to its being confronted and challenged by the kingdom of darkness as it seeks to retain illegally a futile and losing grasp on the kingdoms of this world. St. Peter told the Christians to resist the devil and that he would flee from them. To overcome the devil, St. Paul instructed the Christians in Ephesus about the components they had in Christ Jesus to defeat the onslaughts of the enemy, which would be needed by this church to withstand the devil's most heated attacks during the Great Tribulation. During that time frame between A.D. 66-70, the Ephesian Church was located in the middle of one of the greatest cities within the Roman Empire's Asia Minor where the pagan emperor worship cult and its influence was exceedingly strong, and Christian love was being challenged and waxing cold.[200] St. Paul's words were,

> "Finally, my brethren, be strong in the Lord and in the power of His might. Put on the whole armor of God, that you may be able to stand against the wiles of the devil. For we do not wrestle against flesh and blood, but against principalities, against powers, against the rulers of the darkness of this age, against spiritual hosts of wickedness in the heavenly places. Therefore, take up the whole armor of God, that you may be able to withstand in the evil day, and having done all, to stand. Stand therefore, having girded your waist with truth, having put on the breastplate of righteousness, and having shod your feet with the preparation of the gospel of peace; above all, taking the shield of faith with which you will be able to quench all the fiery darts of the wicked one. And take the helmet of salvation, and the sword of the Spirit, which is the word of God;

---

[199] Matt 12:43-45; and Rev 18:2.

[200] Rev 2:1-7.

praying always with all prayer and supplication in the Spirit, being watchful to this end with all perseverance and supplication for all the saints…"[201]

Satan has not only been defeated by our Lord's work on the cross, in which He disarmed the demonic principalities and powers and made a public spectacle of them, even triumphing over them through the cross, but our Lord also bound Satan at His first century coming so that the devil can no longer deceive the nations unchecked by God and His Church as he once tempted and deceived Adam and Eve in the Garden and mankind after them.[202] St. John in the Revelation of Jesus Christ depicted what Jesus saw in His Spirit, which was His seeing Satan fall as lightening from heaven. This scene was the depiction of the great war between Michael the Archangel and Satan that broke out in heaven sometime around A.D. 66 at the beginning of the Great Tribulation.[203] In this passage in the Revelation of Jesus Christ, we see the sign in heaven of the woman clothed with the sun, which is a picture of the heavenly Jerusalem, the mother of us all, who through the Virgin Mary bears the Christ Child who was to rule all nations with a rod of iron.[204] The red dragon is Satan, who with a third of the heavenly host of rebel angels, tried to destroy the Child (working through Herod the King and others). However, through the ministry and redemptive obedience of Christ, Satan's power over the nations was broken, as Jesus explained prior to His crucifixion, "Now is the judgment of this world; now the ruler of this world will be cast out. And I, if I am lifted up from the earth [a reference to His being crucified], will draw all peoples to Myself."[205]

Further in the Revelation passage, we read that the woman, the Church of Jesus Christ, fled into the wilderness where she was cared for by God for 1260 days (3 ½ years) while enduring a great trial. Prior to this Great Tribulation, the Archangel Michael throws Satan to the earth as lightening from heaven, after

---

[201] Eph 6:10-18.

[202] Col 2:13-15, Rev 20:1-2.

[203] Rev 12:1-17.

[204] C.f., Gen 3:15; Ps(s) 2:9; Rev 2:27; 12:5, 19:15.

[205] John 12:31-33.

which Satan begins his last and most vehement 3 ½ years of focused, destructive havoc upon the children of God, the Church, so as to snuff it completely from the earth. Satan's fight against the church was vehement and deadly because Satan knew that he only had a "short time," 1260 days, to destroy the work of Him who destroyed his rule over the kingdoms of the earth.[206] But, the woman, Zion, the church was protected by God during this troublesome time, even as she walked through the Valley of Death. She overcame the power and lies of the devil by the blood of the Lamb, the word of her people's testimony of faith in Jesus, and they did not love their lives even unto death.[207]

The Lord Jesus and the powers of His Kingdom of Light dispelled the darkness that was a shroud over the world, and eventually the devil's attack destroyed not the Son of God and His Church, but the doomed city of Jerusalem in A.D. 70. It should be noted that Jerusalem was represented in the Revelation by the term "earth" or "land," signifying the former Promised *Land*, as it was called in the Old Testament. Jerusalem absorbed the torrential flood from the dragon's mouth, which ended the Great Tribulation, as Daniel records, calling it the complete shattering of the holy people, which in this case was the end, the desolation, of the Jewish nation as the covenant people of God.[208] These visions from the Revelation concerning the work of Satan under God's Providential hand correspond with the prophet Daniel's words about the fourth kingdom of Rome with its pagan emperors and its most wicked emperor, Nero, who spoke pompously against the Lord of Heaven and persecuted the saints of the Most High.[209] Daniel mentions the saints being given into the hand of this wicked, Satanically inspired emperor for a time and times and half a time (i.e., 3 ½ years or 1260 days or 42 months) until the Ancient of Days came, signifying Jesus's coming on the clouds to save His elect people. At the coming of the Lord with ten thousands of His saints to vanquish His Church's enemies, a judgment was

---

[206] An informative history and explanation of the two casting outs of Satan can be read at footnote #301.

[207] Rev 12:11.

[208] Dan 12:7.

[209] Dan 7:17-28.

made in favor of the saints of the Most High, as Daniel prophesied, and the time came for the saints to possess the Kingdom. The fulfillment of this prophecy in A.D. 70, is what caused the magnificent praise to God at the end of the first major vision in the Revelation.[210]

Beyond the Parousia itself, St. John's Revelation of Jesus Christ, in Rev 20-22, presents what happened after the Parousia of our Lord and after the Great Tribulation: the coming of Christ's Kingdom in great power as He said,[211] and the subsequent and powerful growth of Christ's Kingdom. With Christ's coming in power in A.D. 70, we also have the inauguration of the New Jerusalem growing within the New Heavens and New Earth. As the Lord Jesus returned on the first of the month of Tishri, A.D. 70, St. John in the Revelation of Jesus Christ sees the binding of Satan for a thousand years during the current reign of Christ so that the Devil could no longer deceive the nations regarding Christ, His Lordship, and the successful and victorious growth of His Church, Kingdom, and His salvation.[212] The truth is, Satan can no longer deceive the nations regarding the Gospel of the Kingdom of God. Christ has won and His words and ethics are filling the earth. Every tribe, tongue, and nation is making its way to the Church to hear the word of the Lord as the prophets have spoken.

Today, the only thing retarding the advance of the Kingdom is not the power of Satan, but the impotence of faithless, unbelieving Christians who walk by sight and not by faith in Christ the King and His Lordship. A defeated and bound Satan can only tell lies and lay a shroud of lies over the nations IF the nations and Christians allow him to do so through ignorance, unbelief, or disobedience. Christ has empowered His Church with faith, hope, and love to bring heaven to earth in every aspect of our lives and those of others. The faithless do not speak

---

[210] Rev 11:15-19. The Revelation presents the vision of Christ the King (Rev 1), after which St. John writes what Jesus tells him to say to the seven churches of Asia Minor (Rev 2-3). After this two-chapter epistolary section, St. John gives us the first testimony, in other words the first vision of what is about to happen in the first century regarding Christ's Church and Kingdom (Rev 4-11). The second witness, or testimonial vision is in Rev 12-19, both of which cover the period of the Great Tribulation and Jerusalem's end in A.D. 70.

[211] Matt 16:28; Mark 9:1; Luke 9:27; and Matt 24:30; Mark 13:26; Luke 21:27.

[212] Rev 20:1-3.

the Words of God to themselves and do not diligently drill their children in God's words "when they arise, lie down, or walk by the way," as God commanded us. In other words, the lies of the devil persist only when the "salt loses its savor" in the world. The salt then becomes, as did unbelieving Israel, good for nothing but to be trampled underfoot by unbelieving mankind, as we see in these days.[213]

This is not an irreversible dilemma. The Church must arise and press the crown rights of Christ's Kingdom into every realm of life to obtain "times of refreshing from the Lord"[214] and great blessings of "righteousness, peace, and joy"[215] associated with the Kingdom of God's presence now in these days. This is why every Christian must learn God's design for man to be fruitful, replenish the earth, and exercise Christ's dominion in every realm of life, with faith in the power of Christ's Spirit to prosper this work as God's vicegerents in the earth until Christ comes again. The message of the Revelation of Jesus Christ clearly depicted to a Church under trial that it is a book about the victory and lordship of Christ Jesus and *not* a book that describes how powerful the Devil is, or was, or how powerful and dangerous his puppet, the Image of the Beast, Caesar Nero, was. That is why it is an imperative to preach this Gospel of the Kingdom of God and make disciples of the nations, teaching them to pay obeisance to the Lord Jesus by obeying His commands.

Finally, one needs to know that the binding of Satan and Christ's placing him in the abyss, or bottomless pit, does not mean that he and the demonic forces he led are not active in their lying and deceiving. On the contrary, Satan's binding does mean that the veil of deceit over the nations that had blinded them to the gospel of Jesus Christ in past times has been lifted and that the spiritual impediment that blinded mankind to the truth has been taken out of the way. Having this knowledge allows the Church to preach, teach, and bring grace to the nations in the name of the Lord Jesus, telling them that the Lord reigns over all and that the oppressive nations that exploit the poor and hate liberty and hate God Himself won't last forever. Christians within Christ's Kingdom and

---

[213] Matt 5:13-16.

[214] Acts 3:19-20.

[215] Rom 14:17.

His Church can rejoice that God sees the wicked, no matter how well hidden. And God sees His holy people, knows them, will bless them, will heal them, and will save them as He leads them beside still waters in this life. Christ is building His Church and the gates of Hades shall not be able to withstand the advance.[216] Therefore, a man can confidently and with the promise of God's blessing move forward in life, build a heritage to the glory of God, take to himself a wife, bear as many children as God will give him, work the earth in whatever his hands find to do, worship the Lord, and enjoy God's presence and the Eucharist with his family within the public worship of the Church. This is the righteousness, joy, and peace the Kingdom of God brings to everyone who will believe and obey the Lord who reigns in heaven and takes the earth as His footstool.[217]

The Great Tribulation That Already Was

As the Gospel of the Kingdom was preached in all the world during the first century, as St. Paul wrote, the persecution began to be severe against the Christians.[218] The Jewish converts to Christianity were tempted to turn back to justification by the works of the first covenant's redemptive Law; that is, atonement through the blood of bulls and goats, sacramental circumcision of the male covenant children, and other laws as administered in Jerusalem's temple. Also, both Jewish and Gentile converts to Christianity were being ostracized and martyred among their own people, and even being betrayed to the Roman authorities as seditious and pestiferous Christians by their own families.[219] The temptation tempting all of the converts was to forsake their gathering together as a Church to worship Christ and to hear the Word of the Lord to avoid being noticed or persecuted. The pressure was growing stronger to turn away from the communal love feast of the Eucharist among the gathered brethren on Sundays

---

[216] C.f., Matt 11:12; 16:18.

[217] Isa 66:1; Acts 7:49.

[218] Col. 1:3-6.

[219] Heb 10:23-25; and c.f., Heb 11:32-40 depicting the faithful saints who endured great hardships to follow Christ and enter His Kingdom.

to keep one's job, to buy food and to have company among family and friends. The societal peer and religious pressure and public shaming to renounce Christ was relentless. The time was at hand about which the prophets had spoken called "the Great Distress," or the test upon the entire World, the Roman Empire at that time, which was, as Jesus spoke, the greatest tribulation that had ever been, or would ever be.

Church historian Philip Schaff had so considered this Great Tribulation one of the most significant events in the history of Christ's church that he rewrote his first volume of the History of the Christian Church, Vol 1., to include a major new section on The Great Tribulation, to acknowledge and expound upon this prophesied event, which lasted three and one half years (or as the New Testament prophet, John, called it in the Revelation of Jesus Christ: a time, times, and a half of time; 1290 days; or 42 months. I'll present a summary of Schaff's work on the Great Tribulation below).

During this time, the cruelest Christ-hater that ever lived sat on the throne of the Roman Empire, Caesar Nero, whose number was 666.[220] Although there were many persecutions of the Church, and Augustine named ten of them,[221] it was the Great Distress during the great persecution of Nero and afterwards, his four successors, that was the greatest and most widespread persecution of Christians covering the entire Roman Empire. It focused in its end with laser precision against the seven churches of Asia Minor and upon the city of Jerusalem herself, as we've spoken above, chronicled in Josephus' The Wars of the Jews.[222] Lesser persecutions identified by St. Augustine occurred with decreasing severity and martyrdom numbers during the reigns of Domitian, Trajan, Antoninus, Severus, Maximin, Decius, Valerian, Aurelian and Diocletian and Maximian. After Maximian, Christianity was affirmed as a legal religion and Christians were ordered to be treated benevolently based upon Emperor Constantine's decreeing the Edict of Milan in A.D. 313. Emperor Constantine himself became a Christian, and by A.D. 380, Christ had conquered the Roman Empire, and

---

[220] See Kenneth Gentry's, The Beast of the Revelation.

[221] Augustine, City of God, Book 18, Chapter 52.

[222] Rev 2-3; and The Wars of the Jews, Josephus.

Christianity was its religion. So it is only historical ignorance that would declare that Christ's Kingdom and Jesus' Lordship over the world had no earthly effect in bringing heaven to earth. So severe, however, was the particular persecution of Christians under Nero and his successors that, as Jesus spoke, the time frame was shortened for the chosen people's sake. Jesus described this time frame between A.D. 66 and 70 as "… great tribulation, such as has not been since the beginning of the world until this time, no, nor ever shall be. And unless those days were shortened, no flesh would be saved; but for the elect's sake those days will be shortened."[223]

One of the Church's first deacons, St. Stephen, preached the Kingdom of God and the very soon appearing, or coming, of Christ Jesus, for which he was stoned by the unbelieving and pugilistic Jewish rulers who arranged false witnesses against him. They were recorded as saying, "This man does not cease to speak blasphemous words against this holy place [the Jerusalem Temple] and the law; for we have heard him say that this Jesus of Nazareth will destroy this place and change the customs which Moses delivered to us."[224] St. Stephen rightly spoke of the near destruction of Jerusalem and its temple, as well as Jesus' fulfillment of the Mosaic redemptive laws. Stephen then went too far in the minds of the Jewish rulers when he preached that Jesus as King would return and judge them by destroying their temple and their city. Yet, Stephen was not blaspheming; on the contrary, he was telling the truth that would only be understood by those who were born of the Spirit of God, or born again, or born from above.

The Great Tribulation was a most severe and awful event. By the end of the siege of Jerusalem at the end of the Great Tribulation, over one million Jews were executed by the Romans inside the city itself, which also included a number of Jewish assassins killing their own brethren within the city walls during the siege. The entire city was wiped away along with its temple and its Old Covenant religion. Any remaining Jews were taken by force into slavery. The emperor would not even take to himself the name of the Judeans, which was typical after an emperor conquered a people, because it was shameful to take

---

[223] Matt 24: 21-22; c.f.: Isa 26:20; 54:8; 1 Pet 1:6.

[224] Acts 6:13-14.

the name of a people whose God had forsaken them. Thinking that the Jews and the Christians could be vanquished with one strike of the Roman army's swords, Emperor Vespasian's son, General Titus, lay a siege around the city, starved its inhabitants into surrender, and then sacked the city of Jerusalem, burning it to the ground. Many Church Fathers, theologians, and historians of that time and later have mentioned how the Christians had left the city based on the Word of their prophets and Jesus Christ who had spoken for those inside the city to depart for the mountains when they saw the Roman armies surrounding the city prior to the siege.[225] As Jesus said, those who held to the faith and obeyed His words, enduring to the end of the Great Tribulation, were saved in this life and eternally.

Much historical evidence is documented of how the Christians escaped the doomed city, which St. John referred to as Babylon the Great Whore, as Sodom where the Lord was crucified, and as Egypt.[226] Calling Old Covenant Jerusalem "Sodom" was due to her fornication with Rome and her leaguing with its Emperor Nero, the Beast, and its Image respectively. Moreover she displayed the sins of Sodom that the prophet Ezekiel mentions: pride, fullness of food, and abundance of idleness, along with her neglect of strengthening the hand of the poor and needy.[227] Calling Jerusalem, who had forsaken her Lord, by the name of "Egypt" clearly depicts her as an entity in bondage to the Traditions of the Elders and to her own sins,[228] which made the Law of God of no effect as both Jesus and St. Paul had spoken.[229] Philip Schaff has written that the Christians forsook the city in due time and fled to the town of Pella in the Decapolis, beyond

---

[225] Matt 24:16, Luke 21:21.

[226] Rev 11:8.

[227] Ezek. 16:49.

[228] St. Paul taught the Jews and Converted Gentiles that the Moral Law, the Commandments of God are just, holy, and good, and should always be obeyed (Rom 7:12). St. Paul also taught that the Redemptive Laws of God, which are distinct from the moral laws of God, having to do with ritual, ceremony, and First Covenant sacraments, like circumcision, were abrogated and fulfilled in Christ Jesus. He added that one's continuing to obey them would lead to bondage (Gal 2:4; 4:3, 9, 24-25; 5:1). Christ, His apostles, and all the saints throughout history never denied obedience to God's moral laws. They are the Spirit-breathed tool by which the Church disciples the nations.

[229] Matt 15:6-9; Gal 4:21-27.

the Jordan, in the north of Perea, where King Herod Agrippa II, before whom Paul once stood, opened to them a safe asylum. Also, Eusebius wrote that the Christian flight from Jerusalem took place four years prior to its destruction. Tradition says the leaders of the Christians were led by divine voice or an angel to take flight prior to the 3 ½ years of Great Tribulation that would end in the city's destruction, all of which Eusebius chronicles in detail.[230]

Jesus Christ Distinguished Between the Mark of His Chosen and the "Mark of the Beast"

While addressing the Great Tribulation, we need to address St. John's mention in the Revelation about the mark of the beast. As mentioned earlier, one of the beasts of the Revelation was the Roman Empire. The image of the beast, whose number was that of a man, 666, was Caesar Nero. And it is a fact that Nero did not require anyone to be physically marked in a manner that would signify a person's allegiance to him or to His empire Rome. So, what is this "mark of the beast about which St. John speaks? The answer comes when we look at the concept of a God's marking mankind and its association with redemptive history.

In Scripture and throughout redemptive history, the Lord through his prophets has always marked His people to set them aside for salvation and to distinguish them from those about to be judged. We noted the mark of lamb's blood on the threshold of the household door in Goshen so that the destroying angel would "pass over" the covenant Hebrews and only kill the first born of the idolatrous and rebellious Egyptians, who refused to heed Moses' words to "let God's people go."[231] The mark, as presented many times in Sacred Scripture was either the sign of a loyal and righteous heart and righteous works, or that of a rebellious heart filled with evil thoughts and deeds contrary to the will of

---

[230] Eusebius, Ecclesiastical History, Book III, Chapter 5. Note that the entirety of Book III uses the original sources of Josephus and others to provide a history of those events that fulfilled Jesus' prophecy about His first century coming to save His people and to bring vengeance upon the apostate Jews and their city of Jerusalem and Judea. After Jerusalem's fall, Eusebius describes how the Roman emperors continued to hunt down and destroy any remnants of the line of David so that no ruler ever again would rise from among the Jews.

[231] Ex 12:13.

God. Jeremiah told the Jews that it was their iniquity that marked them, and in another place, he questioned them, asking if they had "marked" and obeyed the Word of the Lord.[232] The prophet Ezekiel wrote that God told the Angel to "Go through the midst of the city, through the midst of Jerusalem, and put a mark on the foreheads of the men who sigh and cry over all the abominations that are done within it."[233] Why the mark on the foreheads? Because the mark signified the righteous thoughts concerning the city of God. The forehead is the seat of the mind, which was marked as loyal and good. The mark on the hands signified the deeds or the works of the man. The mark of God upon the forehead and the hands signified that the man's thoughts, as well as his works were humble, just, holy, and good.[234] Throughout the Revelation of Jesus Christ, when a man's thoughts and deeds were aligned against God and His Christ, he was said to possess the mark of the beast, which meant his loyalties lay with the evil emperor and the unbelieving and persecutory elements of the Jewish and Gentile enemies of Christ.[235]

I mention these passages to move us away from the modern theological thinking among some in the Church who believe that, in the Revelation, a physical mark, or perhaps a computer chip, a social credit card, a vaccine, or some other physical device is what St. John would have been referring to regarding a "mark."[236] In the context of the Revelation, it was during the Great Tribulation that the Jews who died in the faith of Jesus would be those who had not given their allegiance or obedience to the idolatrous dictates of Rome or its emperor. They, therefore, would not have taken the "mark of the beast," which is interpreted as one being wholly conformed to the thoughts, words, and deeds of the Image of the Beast of Rome, which is more specifically the Emperor Nero.

Those who rejected loyalty and obeisance to Rome and to its emperor, risked being ostracized and ridiculed (at the least), or could have been cast out of the

---

[232] Jer 2:22; 23:18.

[233] Ezek 9:3-4.

[234] One sees the "mark of God" upon the foreheads of the righteous in Ezek 9:4,6.

[235] Rev 13:16-17; 14:9, 11; 15:2; 16:2; 19:20. Cf., John 19:14-16.

[236] Ibid.

city of Jerusalem, starved, and then crucified.[237] Rather than conforming to the emperor-worship cult of Rome and rejecting Christ, the Christians would have transformed their minds to prove what was the "perfect will of God" so as to obey Christ, even if it meant certain persecution, confiscation of goods, division of family, and martyrdom.[238]

This mark of the beast was in contradistinction to how the Old Covenant House of Israel was to live. Yahweh God through Moses taught the Children of Israel,

> "Therefore you shall lay up these words of mine in your heart and in your soul, and <u>bind them as a sign on your hand</u>, and they shall be as <u>frontlets between your eyes</u> [signifying the forehead]. You shall teach them to your children, speaking of them when you sit in your house, when you walk by the way, when you lie down, and when you rise up. And you shall write them on the doorposts of your house and on your gates, that your days and the days of your children may be multiplied in the land of which the Lord swore to your fathers to give them, like the days of the heavens above the earth."[239]

To obey the Lord Jesus in works of faith, hope, and love signified not only that the Covenant keeper was marked by the Lord, but it also signified the entire heavens and earth to the Jew, hence Moses' use of the words referring to Yahweh's blessing upon their obedience as "like the days of heaven on earth."

---

[237] Note: Contemporary commentary throwing the meaning of this text forward to current times, that calls, for example in 2022, the covid vaccines the "mark of the beast," necessitates saying that anyone who received the vaccines has "received the mark of the beast." This is just one example of contemporary *Last Days Madness*. Full adherence to this understanding of that text does not merely mean that the commentators are relinquishing vaccine recipients to those who cannot buy or sell without this mark. It, in adherence to the understanding of the Revelation means the defining of a covid vaccine recipient as not only "marked by" Satan but as *belonging* to him. And that is ridiculous. A mark is like a cattle branding upon the mind and the deeds, which depicts ownership. That is a misapplication of this metaphor.

[238] Rom. 12:1-2.

[239] Deut 11:18-20; c.f., Deut 6:6-8.

Likewise, in the first century, God spoke to His angel to mark the righteous prior to the destruction of the Roman armies and the Great City of Jerusalem. In Revelation 7:2, we see: "Then I saw another angel ascending from the east, having the seal of the living God. And he cried with a loud voice to the four angels to whom it was granted to harm the earth and the sea, **3** saying, "Do not harm the earth, the sea, or the trees till we have sealed the servants of our God on their foreheads." **4** And I heard the number of those who were sealed. One hundred *and* forty-four thousand of all the tribes of the children of Israel *were* sealed." Note in verse 4 that all of those faithful Jews coming out of the apostasy of Jerusalem were ordained by God to be marked and saved. St. John is revealing symbolically, not literally, that 12,000 were saved out of each of the twelve tribes of Israel totaling the perfect number of 144,000. These 144,000 were the same symbolic number of converted Jews that we would see in St. John's second vision of the Revelation wherein the symbolically numbered 144,000, all marked by the Lord on their forehead, are standing atop Mount Zion, the New Jerusalem with Christ Jesus by their side.

The wicked, on the other hand, bore the mark of the evil one and his image, the emperor, on their foreheads, signifying their thoughts, and on their hands, signifying their dead evil works.[240] The unbelievers and those who forsook Yahweh for apostasy for whatever reason, including cowardice, allowed themselves to be marked to avoid persecution and ostracism.[241] Those receiving the mark of Rome's allegiance sought to save their lives by avoiding persecution; however, as Jesus warned, they lost their lives forever.[242] They tossed away their faith in Yahweh incarnate, Jesus Christ, traded their salvation and blessing to be conformed to pagan Rome and to the rule and Traditions of the Elders taught by the hypocritical Pharisees. These Pharisees preached Moses and the Prophets, but did not obey them. It is written in 2 Tim 2:19, "Nevertheless the solid foundation of God stands, having this seal: "The Lord knows those who are His," and, "Let everyone who names the name of Christ depart from iniquity."

---

[240] Rev 13:16; 14:9-11; 15:2; 16:2; 19:20; 20:4.

[241] Rev 13:17.

[242] Matt 16:25.

Church Historian Schaff Summarizes the First Century's Great Tribulation

Philip Schaff presents an extensive study and comprehensive look at this Great Tribulation between A.D. 66 and 70. He revised his prior work on Volume 1 based on his accepting the view of the early dating of Revelation; that is, being written prior to A.D.70. [243] He considered this as necessary to understanding the message of the Revelation itself. According to Schaff:

> "Christ spoke of this great tribulation that would have its focus on Jerusalem and Judea, and there was never a more alarming state of society. The horrors of the French Revolution were confined to one country, but the tribulation of the six years preceding the destruction of Jerusalem extended over the whole Roman empire and embraced wars and rebellions, frequent and unusual conflagrations, earthquakes and famines and plagues, and all sorts of public calamities and miseries untold. It seemed indeed that the world, shaken to its very center was coming to a close, and every Christian must have felt that the prophecies of Christ were being fulfilled before his eyes. For John, the Neronian persecution behind him, horrible persecution and wars before him, the destruction of the Holy City, who has played the whore with the nations upon him, and the triumph of the Church of Jesus Christ just a short time away…this was a Revelation of the times, for the times, and for an encouragement to the Christian brethren. Jerusalem crucified the Lord, Rome beheaded and crucified his chief apostles and plunged the whole Roman church into a baptism of blood. Vatican Hill was the Golgotha of the West. Rome had now rushed headlong into deadly conflict with the new religion. Nero, the Caesar during the martyrdom of Peter and Paul in A.D. 64. Paul, the most noble, and Nero one of the basest and vilest of tyrants. He donned animal skins and raped male and female prisoners,

---

[243] Schaff, Philip, <u>History of the Christian Church</u>, Vol 1: The Great Tribulation, 1901.

he had an insane passion for popular applause; he played on the lyre; he sung his odes at supper, he drove his chariots in the circus; he appeared on stage and compelled men of the highest rank to portray the obscenest of the Greek myths. Josephus speaks of the crimes of Nero, but not of any persecution of Jews at the time…only Christians. There is scarcely another period in history so full of vice, corruption, and disaster as the six years between the Neronian persecution and the destruction of Jerusalem."[244]

During the Great Tribulation, Nero was "the man of sin" who allegedly started the fire that burned much of Rome, causing much of the city to lay in ruins. The cause of the fire is still a mystery; however, some thought Nero wanted to burn Rome to the ground and start a new city, Neropolis, bearing his namesake. To divert the general suspicion of incendiarism from himself, Nero blamed the hated Christians, who were beginning to be distinguished as a dangerous offshoot from the Jews due to St. Paul's success in Rome. As such, many thought Judaism and Christianity were one. This launched an unprecedented carnival of blood in Rome under Nero in which Peter and Paul died. This murderous time included Nero's covering Christians with pitch and oil and lighting them afire to light his parties and the city ways. Burning alive was the punishment for incendiarism, which took place on Vatican Hill in the Neronian Gardens. Tacitus, as portrayed here in one of his works, knew that the Christians were innocent of incendiarism, and, in spite of his cold stoicism, he pitied the Christians for being slaughtered not for the public good, but for the ferocity of a wicked tyrant—Nero.

> "… fastened the guilt and inflicted the most exquisite tortures on a class hated for their abominations, called Christians by the populace. Christus, from whom the name had its origin, suffered the extreme penalty during the reign of Tiberius at the hands of one of our procurators, Pontius Pilatus, and a most mischievous superstition, thus checked for the moment, again

---

[244] Ibid.

broke out not only in Judæa, the first source of the evil, but even in Rome, where all things hideous and shameful from every part of the world find their centre and become popular. Accordingly, an arrest was first made of all who pleaded guilty; then, upon their information, an immense multitude was convicted, not so much of the crime of firing the city, as of hatred against mankind. [He then describes the torture of Christians] Mockery of every sort was added to their deaths. Covered with the skins of beasts, they were torn by dogs and perished, or were nailed to crosses, or were doomed to the flames and burnt, to serve as a nightly illumination, when daylight had expired. Nero offered his gardens for the spectacle, and was exhibiting a show in the circus, while he mingled with the people in the dress of a charioteer or stood aloft on a car. Hence, even for criminals who deserved extreme and exemplary punishment, there arose a feeling of compassion; for it was not, as it seemed, for the public good, but to glut one man's cruelty, that they were being destroyed."[245]

The Jews themselves instigated hatred of the Christians via lies, false witnesses, and false accusations.[246] John the Apostle was exiled to Patmos under Nero, where he would be given from Christ Himself the Revelation of Jesus Christ. Says Gibbons on Nero, "Those who survey with a curious eye the revolutions of mankind, may observe that the gardens and circus of Nero on the Vatican, which were polluted with the blood of the first Christians, have been rendered still more famous by the triumph and by the abuse of that persecuted religion. On the same spot, a temple, which far surpasses the ancient glories of the capital, has been since erected by the Christian pontiffs, who, deriving their claim of universal dominion from a humble fisherman of Galilee, have succeeded to the throne of the Caesars, given laws to the Barbarian conquerors of Rome,

---

[245] Aleteia, Web Article, *Ancient History is not Quiet Concerning Jesus Tacitus Attests*, quoting Tacitus from his <u>Annals</u>. https://aleteia.org/2019/04/08/ ancient-history-is-not-quiet-about-jesus-as-tacitus-attests/

[246] Acts 6:8-14.

and extended their spiritual jurisdiction from the coast of the Baltic to the shores of the Pacific Ocean."[247] The Kingdom of God came in power as Jerusalem fell, which marked a definitive beginning of the end for the Roman Empire, which shall never rise again.

From the Revelation and from accounts taken from Josephus' The Wars of the Jews, Schaff points out that Rome is seen as the beast arising from the west out of the Mediterranean Sea and that the number of the Image of the Beast, 666, correlated with Caesar Nero.[248] Chilton also has made the case that the other beast from the land, signifying the Promised Land, was Jerusalem, a beast in lamb's clothing yet speaking the demonically inspired words of the Dragon, which represented pagan Rome. This depicted Jerusalem's apostasy based on its denial of the words of Moses, the original biblical faith.[249] "Orthodox Christianity *alone* is the true continuation and fulfillment of Old Testament religion (see Matt. 5:17-20; 15:1-9; Mark 7:1-13; Luke 16:29-31; John 8:42-47).[250] This denial of the faith of Yahweh and the commensurate disbelief in His Son, Jesus, was evidenced, for example, with the Jews' words at the crucifixion of Christ, "We have no king but Caesar," and their most self-condemning words of all, "His blood be upon us and our children." The Jewish nation was to represent Yahweh God and the words of His Christ, yet they aligned themselves to pagan Rome, thus worshipping the beast from the Sea.[251] The *image* of that beast was a man, a Caesar whose name, when spelled with Hebrew letters totaled the number 666, when all of the consonants in his name in the Hebrew rendering were summed (NeRoN KeSaR).[252]

Tacitus described the political environment during the Great Tribulation beginning his account after the death of Nero,

---

[247] Gibbons, Rise and Fall of the Roman Empire, Chapter 16.

[248] Rev 13:1-10.

[249] Chilton, Days of Vengeance, pp. 335-344.

[250] Ibid, page 337.

[251] Rev 13:4-5.

[252] Rev 13:11-18, also see Gentry's, The Beast of the Revelation.

"I proceed to a work rich in disasters, full of atrocious battles, of discord and rebellion, yea, horrible even in peace. Four princes (Galba, Otho, Vitellius, Domitian) killed by the sword; three civil wars, several foreign wars; and mostly raging at the same time. The most unfortunate country in that period was Palestine...the tragedy of Jerusalem prefigures in miniature the final judgment, represented in the eschatological discourses of Christ in Matthew 24. The temple burned and destroyed, and not one stone left upon another. James the Just stoned by the Jews in Jerusalem and thrown from the pinnacle of the temple. In A.D. 67, Vespasian opened the campaign by overrunning Galilee with an army of 60,000 men. Rome hindered him from completing the battles. Nero killed himself, Galba, Otho, and Vitellius followed him...the latter being taken out of a dog's kennel in Rome while drunk, dragged through the streets, and shamefully put to death. Vespasian was declared emperor in A.D. 69. Vespasian's son Titus became general to execute the war on Jerusalem. 80,000 trained soldiers were stationed upon Mt. Scopas and the adjoining Mt. Olivet in full view of the city and the temple...the Valley of Kedron separated the besiegers from the besieged. In Apr A.D.70, immediately after the Passover, the siege began. The Romans crucified nearly 500 Jews per day, and during the famine caught a woman roasting her child for food. The cries of mothers and children were horrendous.[253]

Schaff records events that assist one in concluding that the Jews in trying to save their whole heavens and earth of their world, actually found themselves fighting against Christ Himself and hastening their doom:

"History records no other instance of such obstinate resistance, such desperate bravery and contempt of death. The Jews fought, not only for civil liberty, life, and their native land...

---

[253] Tacitus, HISTORIES, I.c.2.

even in this state of horrible degeneracy, infused into them an almost superhuman power of endurance. Daily sacrifices ceased on 17 July A.D.70 due to all-hands needed for defense of the city and the temple. The last and bloodiest sacrifice was the Romans entering the temple (the abomination that makes desolate) and slaughtered thousands of Jews who were clinging to the horns of the altar crowding around it. Titus wanted to save the temple, but the fires of the city seemed spurred on higher by a higher decree. Titus' armies moved into the Holy of Holies to try and arrest the rebels. Then, by a soldier claiming divine inspiration, a firebrand was hurled through the golden gate of the temple. When the flames arose, the Jews let forth with a hideous yell and tried to extinguish the fire. No false messiahs were providing comfort, and the Romans were now wanting the rebels to feel the full force of their rage. The temple was burned and destroyed on the 10th of August A.D.70, the first of Tishri, the same day of the year according to tradition the first temple was destroyed by Nebuchadnezzar. The Loud shout of victory from the legions, and the wailings of the people now surrounded by fire and sword…the echoes from the mountains around increased the deafening roar. Jerusalem was raised to the ground. The ground wasn't visible due to the innumerable corpses. The Romans planted their eagles on the ruins and made sacrifices to them, and proclaimed Titus Imperator with the greatest acclamation of joy. Titus declared that God, by special providence aided the Romans and drove the Jews from their impregnable strongholds. Josephus went through the entire war: first as Governor of Galilee and general of the Jewish army, then as prisoner of Vespasian, finally as companion of Titus and mediator between the Romans and the Jews. Vespasian retained Jerusalem as his private property. The people were reduced to poverty. No magistrate, no temple, no sacrifice, nothing, totally stripped, divorced from Yahweh God, and disinherited from the Kingdom of God.

When Jerusalem was rebuilt as a Christian city, its bishop was raised to the dignity of one of the four patriarchs of the East. This final act of the Great Tribulation, the assured sign of the Son of Man's reigning over all in heaven with all authority and power separated apostate Judaism from Christianity forever."[254]

As Schaff concludes his account of the Great Tribulation that was and will never be again, he says,

"The rupture was consummated by the thunderbolt of divine omnipotence. God himself destroyed the house in which he thus far dwelt. The cords of the infant Church of Jesus Christ were cut, and she arose to a sense of maturity. The scaffolding of the Old Testament theocratic fabric came down, and the New Jerusalem stood strong and tall and began filling the earth… The Christians appeared as genuine Jews, as spiritual children of Abraham, who followed Messiah Jesus. The Jewish-Christian and Gentile-Christian assemblies were now fused as one holy, catholic, and apostolic church."[255]

Christ's Appearing, His Parousia, His Coming in the Clouds

The Great Tribulation ended with Christ's coming in the clouds on that Great Day of the Lord,[256] an event known as His Appearing,[257] or His Parousia. It was characterized by the coming of Christ in the clouds with all of His saints, while bringing the Kingdom of God to earth in power and inaugurating the Thousand-Year Reign of Christ the King. This Parousia[258] also inaugurated the

---

[254] Schaff, Ibid.

[255] Ibid.

[256] Matt 24:30; 26:64; c.f., Ps(s) 104:3.

[257] Matt 24:30; 2 Tim. 4:1.

[258] Matt 24:27, 37, 39; 1 Cor 15:23; 1 Thess 2:19; 5:23; James 5:8; 1 John 2:28.

New Heavens and New Earth, which continues to grow and fill the earth to this day.[259] Again, we must mention that just because we are declaring that Christ came in the clouds in the first century, as He spoke, that conclusion does not in any way deny the Church's dogma of Christ's "Second Coming." As stated earlier, there were many comings of the Lord in time and in history, and one of the greatest of these appearances, or comings of the Lord, was His Parousia in the first century. At that event, one did not see Christ Jesus physically in the sky, but one noted the impacts of His reign and the fulfillment of what He had prophesied while He was speaking and acting on earth.

One sees the most vivid picture of the coming of the Lord as King of Kings and Lord of Lords at the end of the Great Tribulation in the Revelation of Jesus Christ.[260] The language used to describe Christ's coming, or His appearance, is that He comes with His white-clothed saints and angelic armies of heaven. This is why He is called the "Lord of Sabaoth [not Sabbath]," or "Lord of Armies," or "Lord of Hosts." The saints who had died and especially those who were martyred for the faith during the Great Tribulation came with Him as promised.[261] Our Lord Jesus came with His armies to slay those who fought against His Church, depicted symbolically as the "woman" in Rev 12, who was being protected and nourished by Yahweh God during this time of great distress. Those were the days of God's vengeance, and mankind's evil works abounded in every place due to the devil's being cast out of heaven and being thrown to the earth to wreak havoc for a short time.[262] The result of the mass carnage at the end of those days of vengeance set the course of the "supper of the great God," beginning with the angel's call to all the birds of the air to come eat the flesh of those who died as a result of having made war against Christ and His people. This included the False Prophet (unbelieving Jerusalem) and the Image of the Beast (who was Nero and the successor emperors themselves).[263]

---

[259] Rev 20:1-6.

[260] Rev 19:11-21.

[261] Ps(s) 149:5-9; Matt 19:28; Luke 22:30.

[262] See Josephus, The Wars of the Jews.

[263] Rev 19:11-21.

Interpretations of the Thousand-Year Reign of Christ

As mentioned earlier, the Thousand-Year Reign is figurative in nature as opposed to a literal period of one thousand years. This is why some interpreters of prophecy since the second century A.D. have thought the Lord would return in the year A.D. 1000 or would return sometime in the future and reign for a literal 1000 years. Either conclusion cannot be systematically substantiated from Scripture and has never been the dogmatic position of the Church. Many interpreters of the "thousand-year" passage in Revelation 20, however, agree, including the Catholic Church, with a symbolic interpretation of the thousand-year time span. This places this interpretation into the eschatological category of "amillennial," meaning literally without a millennium, or not a literal millennium of time. Being amillennial as to eschatology certainly does not mean one doesn't believe in a one-thousand-year reign of Christ. Churches that hold to amillennialism have historically believed the number of years within Christ's reign is symbolic and will continue until the end of this age. There are many flavors of amillennialism.

TThere are pure amillennialists, primarily among the Catholics, Anglicans, and Orthodox Churches, who believe the Thousand-Year reign of Christ is symbolic as to time and is not a time in which Christianity will fill the earth effectively and potently before Christ's return. The amillennialist does believe that Jesus Christ will return after His Thousand-Year Reign to judge the living and the dead. Post-millennialism, another notable and growing eschatological belief, holds to the doctrine defined as our Lord returning after His current *symbolic* thousand-year reign, hence the term "post-millennial." The historical post-millennialist view also holds that during this Reign of Christ, the vast majority of people living will be saved, and the earth will be filled with the glory of the Lord, Christianized, as His reign continues until all things non-Christian are placed under Christ's feet. Many Christians, especially among Protestant Presbyterians, hold to post-millennialism, which, in the 17th century, was often referred to as "the Puritan hope."[264] This author embraces the symbolism of the millennium

---

[264] For details on post-millennialism, see Gentry's, He Shall Have Dominion, and Boetner's, The Millennium.

of amillennialism as well as the potent Christianizing of the earth taught in post-millennialism, which includes an eventual Christian-dominated world prior to the release of Satan prior to the expiration of this Thousand-Year Reign of Christ and His final return to judge the living and the dead. This Christianizing of the earth, it must be noted, will not come about via ecclesiastical or political militaristic power or social engineering, but, as Zechariah prophesied, it will happen by the work of the Holy Spirit of God working through the Church in her discipleship of the nations and through her people working in every sphere of life: families, churches, and States.

So, one can see that these eschatologies have more implications than merely a literal or figurative sense as to the number of years associated with Christ's reign. Many amillennialists, who rightly hold to a figurative number of years for Christ's reign, do not see Christ, His Church, and the power of the living Spirit of God as having any victorious results on earth other than the saving of some souls. This eschatology fails to incorporate the words of the prophets that speak to the earth being filled progressively with the Word and blessings of God prior to Christ's return. This view sees Christ's Reign as spiritual in nature and sees the Church of Jesus Christ as somewhat floundering during Christ's reign. This system seems to deny the progressive, visible, and inevitable growth of the Kingdom of God in the earth that Jesus taught in His parables, and as what is clearly the teaching of the Old Testament prophets. Jesus taught that the Kingdom of God is like leaven, which is kneaded into dough to make it progressively, visibly, powerfully and inevitably rise. He also said that the Kingdom is like a mustard seed, the smallest of all seeds, but one that grows visibly and powerfully over time into a sprawling tree in which all of the fowl of the air may rest in its branches. One can deduce from Sacred Scripture as well as historical evidence, that the growth of the number of Christians and their influence in all of the earth will be progressive, incremental, and visible in every realm of life, and inevitable as God visibly places all of Christ Jesus' enemies under His feet. This writer, therefore, would reject the noted impotent earthly implications of the amillennial view, believing instead in the earthly victory of Christianity filling the earth as do the post-millennialists. Many in this post-millennial school of thought hold that every man, woman, and child on the earth will either be Christian, or will feign belief in Christianity, both of which will make for a peaceful and orderly world culture of blessing prior to the end of Christ's current reign.

Contrary to the amillennial and post-millennialist views is dispensationalism, which holds that Christ's Thousand-Year Reign is still to come in the future when He comes again at the Second Coming. This system of eschatological doctrine made popular in the early 19th century by the Schofield Reference and Dake's Study Bibles, Moody Bible Institute, and Dallas Theological Seminary, holds that redemptive history consists of multiple dispensations in which God deals with His people in different ways, as opposed to one covenantal, manner. This system also erroneously holds that there is a continuing covenant with the Jewish nation and a different New Covenant with Christians: sort of an Old and New Covenant running side by side, if you will. Dispensationalism fails to see the fulfillment of Jesus' prophecies in the first century fall of Jerusalem. The dispensationalist would say there will need to be a replication of the first century environment for prophecies to be fulfilled. This would require a revised Roman Empire, a rebuilt Jerusalem temple complete with redemptive sacrifices, a restored Levitical priesthood, and a Great Tribulation to come. Dispensationalists believe in three options as to when Jesus Christ will return: 1. before the Great Tribulation, 2. during the middle of the tribulation, or 3. after the tribulation. Dispensationalism is a novel, disjointed set of "end times" beliefs that have no thread of continuity within them and that do not align with the body of Sacred Scripture.

One other eschatological system of thought associated, too, with the Thousand-Year Reign of Christ is called preterism. Preterism teaches that all prophecy has been fulfilled in A.D. 70, and that there will not be a subsequent and final return of Christ; that is, no Second Coming. This author's response is that since the days of our Lord's apostles, the Church has dogmatically declared that Christ will return again after this Thousand-Year Reign to judge the living and the dead.[265] Preterism is a system of eschatology that denies the final return

---

[265] Some passages in 1 Cor 15 and in Rev 20 depict a final return of our Lord after this current reign of Christ to judge the living and the dead as the Church has dogmatically spoken in its Creeds and Catechisms.

of Christ and the bodily resurrection of the dead. The preterist would believe that everything spoken of in the Bible has come to pass, including Christ's final return. The Preterist does not see multiple comings of our Lord and would not agree with the position of a final coming at the end of His current reign. Some have humorously referred to this system of eschatology as "post-everything-ism."

To summarize a credible biblical eschatology, one needs to combine the analogy of Scripture (comparing hard to understand Scripture with passages of Scripture that are easier to interpret) and the analogy of faith (adhering to the dogmatic and doctrinal conclusions of the Church throughout the past two thousand years). One also needs to realize that the Church is not dogmatic on every jot and tittle of eschatology. So, one needs to continue learning and not be overly dogmatic other than where the Church has spoken to be so. In applying the analogy of faith and that of Scripture, one can conclude that Christ came in salvation and judgment at the end of the first century Great Tribulation and established his Thousand-Year Reign, interpreted as a symbolic thousand-year time span. This position aligns in many ways with historic amillennialism and post-millennialism.[266] Christ as King and Lord currently reigns over a growing Christianity of righteousness, peace, and joy in all of the earth over time until all of the world obeys and sees rightly that Jesus Christ is Yahweh God and Lord over all. Mankind will acknowledge this truth whether in truth or feigned, thus ushering in worldwide blessing and eventually the laying down of weapons of war among the nations. When all of Christ's enemies are subdued and the world is Christianized from the least to the greatest, then the Lord shall return from heaven to judge the living and the dead. This position recognizes the dogmatic creeds of the Church. So, this writer's conclusions are eclectic in nature as drawn from reflections from Scripture and from evidence from Church Tradition and historical events throughout redemptive history. These general sources of reflection give one a natural eschatology of hope and Christian victory. This motivates one to fulfill the cultural mandate and to live one's life under the Lordship of Christ now, while living with great joy, awaking daily to do good works of faith, hope, and love, while building and making grace-filled, God-glorifying

---

[266] E.g., St. Augustine, Dr. B.B. Warfield, Dr. R.J. Rushdoony, Dr. Gary North, Dr. David Chilton, Dr. Greg Bahnsen, and Dr. Kenneth Gentry, to name a few.

contributions in the world.[267] This hope of the victory of Christ's Reign empowers and motivates one to labor with rational optimism under the reigning King Jesus Christ, whose Kingdom is an everlasting kingdom and is filling the earth. The Lord reigns, let the earth rejoice, and let the multitude of islands be glad.

The First Resurrection

Since our Lord's appearing in A.D. 70, one must address the First Resurrection of the just ones and the Lake of Fire for the sinners. The First Resurrection, in this author's opinion, seems to be an event that ties together the prophecies of Daniel and St. John in the Revelation, as well as other relevant Old and New Testament passages. A discussion of the First Resurrection also by necessity brings up the nature of the Final Judgment to come after the Thousand-Year Reign of Christ expires, addressed in full in *Table 5*.

God gave His people the same message throughout redemptive history beginning in the Garden with the Protoevangelium: there is life beyond death from the original sin of Adam, and this eternal, abundant, restored life would come through the Second Adam, Christ Jesus, the Seed of the Woman, the Blessed Virgin Mary.[268] Christ died for the sins of many and was raised from the dead. The Apostle St. Paul has said, "…if we have been united together in the likeness of His [Christ's] death, certainly we also shall be in the likeness of His resurrection.[269] God is the God of the living, Who would not allow His Christ to see corruption, and neither would he allow His holy people to physically die without hope."[270] The resurrection of the dead, both the First Resurrection as well as the general resurrection at the Return of Christ are both established on that promised and fulfilled glorious and powerful Resurrection of Jesus Christ from the dead.

---

[267] See Marcellus Kik, An Eschatology of Victory.

[268] Rom 5:12-19.

[269] Rom 6:5.

[270] Ps(s) 16:10.

As for the House of Israel, recall that Daniel was given to know that in the "latter days." For example, God would deliver His people through the Great Tribulation: "…everyone who is found written in the book…[And] many of those who sleep in the dust of the earth shall awake, some to everlasting life, some to shame and everlasting contempt.[271] Those who are wise shall shine like the brightness of the firmament, and those who turn many to righteousness like the stars forever and ever."[272] The sense of Daniel's prophecy is that there would be believers in the Christ to come since the days of Adam and from among the Jewish people who would be delivered through the first century great distress, either by dying for their faith (martyrdom) in Jesus, or by surviving the tribulation while holding fast to their faith.[273] Those who would have died in the faith, presumably from the days of Adam until Christ's Parousia, would be raised from the dead to everlasting life at Christ Jesus' Parousia. To be specific, those believers would have partaken of the First Resurrection at Christ's Parousia, which was the raising of all of those who died in the faith of Jesus holding fast to Him[274] awaiting His victorious Parousia. The rest of those who had died outside of faith in Christ Jesus, would not rise again until Christ's return to judge the living and dead of all time, an event that would occur after the Thousand-Year Reign expires.[275] Yahweh then through His messenger told Daniel to seal the book until the time of the end of the Jewish people, a term synonymous with the end of the 70 weeks as presented earlier. The book that was sealed was the same book that Jesus was found worthy to unseal as recorded in Rev 5. When those outside the faith are to be raised, they, according to Daniel, would be raised to everlasting contempt

---

[271] Dan 10:14.

[272] Dan 12:1-3.

[273] Ibid, and Dan 12:13.

[274] Those saints who had been martyred for the faith of Christ were awaiting Christ's victory at His Parousia. We see these saints in Rev 6: 9: "When He opened the fifth seal, I saw under the altar the souls of those who had been slain for the word of God and for the testimony which they held. 10 And they cried with a loud voice, saying, 'How long, O Lord, holy and true, until You judge and avenge our blood on those who dwell on the earth?' 11 Then a white robe was given to each of them; and it was said to them that they should rest a little while longer, until both the number of their fellow servants and their brethren, who would be killed as they were, was completed."

[275] Rev 20:4-6.

and perdition. Daniel was blessedly promised that he would rest with His people and would arise to his inheritance at the end of the days of His people. We do know from Sacred Scripture that when Jesus arose from the dead, He took those in Paradise, or Abraham's Bosom, with Him to reside in His heavenly Kingdom and to await their participation in the First Resurrection. In addition, those saints in Christ who had either died since the Resurrection of Christ or who were alive persevering in the faith during His Parousia would also partake of the First Resurrection. Those in Paradise were those faithful Jews and God-fearing Gentiles, who had died prior to Christ's resurrection and we're awaiting the Messiah to set them free to abide with Him in the heavenly Kingdom.

Resurrection unto life is a strong theme throughout redemptive history. Ezekiel, speaking also of the Resurrection, provides a vision of a valley of dry bones coming to life by the breath (Spirit) of God and becoming an exceedingly great army.[276] Ezekiel also prophesied that Yahweh God would open their graves and cause them to come up from their graves and bring them into the land of Israel, the Church, the New Jerusalem in the inaugurated New Heavens and New Earth. God says He would place His Spirit within them and place them in their own land. These prophecies have everything to do with the abundant life-giving, spiritual yet visible and transformational, Kingdom of God on earth that would fill the earth under the Lordship of Messiah Jesus.

The Christians from among the converted Jews and Gentiles who passed through the Great Tribulation were instructed, as was mentioned earlier, by Jesus in the Revelation to overcome by the blood of the Lamb of God, the faithful word of their testimony of Jesus as Lord and King, not loving their lives even if their testimony of Jesus would lead to their physical deaths through martyrdom.[277] The promise via the words of the prophet Daniel and through St. John in the Revelation of Jesus Christ was that these persevering overcomers in Christ would partake of the First Resurrection and avoid the Second Death.[278] The Second Death is the eternal and final judgment of being cast into the Lake of

---

[276] Ezek 37.

[277] Rev. 12:10-12.

[278] Rev 2:11; 20:6, 14.

Fire because of one's name not being found in the Lamb's Book of Life. To the Jew, his continued faith in and obedience to the words of Yahweh God, which in the first century meant faith in and obedience to Jesus Christ, gave promise to his rising from the dead to eternal life in the Kingdom of the Heavens at the end of the days of First Covenant Jerusalem. The believing Jew (and called and chosen from among the Gentiles), according to Daniel and the words of Christ's apostles, would either rise from the dead at the Lord's Parousia and enjoy the bliss of the heavenly Kingdom, or if alive at the coming of the Lord, would as St. Paul prophetically said, "meet the Lord in the air" (symbolically speaking) and walk from then on as seated in heavenly places in Christ.[279]

The faithful Christians knew that if they were to die prior to Christ's Parousia, they would not only join Christ and the angels in heaven, but join them both as they return in the Parousia coming upon the twelve tribes of Israel and judging them. Those living at the time of Christ's appearing at the end of the Great Tribulation, would be changed and would shine as the firmament in heaven as Daniel prophesied. Those alive at Christ's Parousia would from that day on reign as kings and priests of God while alive, even though they would eventually physically die. This is why St. John wrote of Jesus saying that those who would believe in Christ while they yet lived, would never die.[280]

And What about the "Rapture?"

The idea of this First Resurrection provides a forum for addressing the contemporary fringe doctrine believed among most Protestant fundamentalists: the Rapture. They believe that this event was spoken of in Paul's letter to the Thessalonians in 1 Thess 4:17-18, considered to be a secret catching away of the saints prior to a future Great Tribulation.[281] The Rapture teaching is neither a historical teaching of the Church, nor has it ever been generally accepted by

---

[279] Eph 2:4-7; 1 Thess 4:13—5:11; and c.f. 1 Cor 15:51-53.

[280] John 11:25-27.

[281] 1 Thess 4:17-18; Eph 2:4-7; John 8:51-52.

the Church. It is a rather novel and contemporary teaching, only seen in the Protestant fundamentalist churches as part of their dispensational eschatology since the mid-1800s. It is NOT dogmatically accepted by the Church.

This author would argue that Christ's return in A.D. 70, was a spiritual yet very real event that occurred as a reward, as Daniel wrote, for those who had borne testimony to Christ and who had either died in the Lord prior to His coming in A.D. 70, or who were still alive at His coming. This being "caught up," from which is where the Latin term "rapture" is derived, is referring to the Lord's rewarding and placing His people in heavenly places as they walked as His own in this world. At that time, the Christian overcomer who was alive at Christ's first century Parousia would walk and shine as a king and priest in this life as a subject of Jesus the Lord and King of all.[282]

These enigmatic words of St. Paul were meant to comfort the Thessalonians, who were under severe persecution by the unbelieving Jews and Romans. They were losing heart that so many of their numbers were being severely persecuted and martyred. The epistle to the Thessalonians should be read noting that there were no chapter divisions between chapters four and five. It should also be noted that St. Paul, as chapter five begins, tells the Thessalonians that this Day of the Lord would not overtake them unawares, thus signifying to them the nearness and relevance of Christ's soon-coming upon the first century world.

> 1 Thessalonians 4 13 But I do not want you to be ignorant, brethren, concerning those who have fallen asleep, lest you sorrow as others who have no hope. 14 For if we believe that Jesus died and rose again, even so God will bring with Him those who sleep [have died] in Jesus. 15 For this we say to you by the word of the Lord, that we who are alive and remain until the coming of the Lord will by no means precede those who are asleep [dead]. 16 For the Lord Himself will descend from heaven with a shout, with the voice of an archangel, and with the trumpet of God. And the dead in Christ will rise first. 17

---

[282] Rev 1:6; 5:10.

Then we who are alive and remain shall be caught up together with them in the clouds to meet the Lord in the air. And thus we shall always be with the Lord. 18 Therefore comfort one another with these words.

Keep in mind that Paul's epistle continues from Chapter 4:18 to Chapter 5 (below) without a chapter break in the original Greek manuscripts. The original Greek manuscripts also were without chapter headings that try to interpret the narratives in chapters 4 and 5, contrary to our modern translations. One can see that St. Paul is telling the Thessalonians that the times and seasons of the Lord's descending with a shout at the last trumpet was about to happen, which were events that we clearly see written at the end of the two visions in the Revelation of Jesus Christ.[283] This being caught up as sitting in heavenly places made those living saints at Christ's appearing in A.D. 70 shine as the stars of heaven among those living in the world. Is it any wonder that Christianity filled the Roman Empire and consumed it within 280 years after Christ's resurrection? The Church's unparalleled growth during this period was no doubt a result of the effectual power of a fervent Church growing and bringing all things in this world under the Lordship of Christ. The Church was fulfilling the Cultural Mandate under its Head, Jesus Christ, Who was now ruling and reigning as were His people in life in this world.

5 1But concerning the times and the seasons, brethren, you have no need that I should write to you. 2 For you yourselves know perfectly that the day of the Lord so comes as a thief in the night. 3 For when they say, "Peace and safety!" then sudden

---

[283] In the Revelation of Jesus Christ, one first sees the vision of Christ the King, then the letters to the seven churches followed by two extended visions that are two similar witnesses of the same events. The first extended vision begins at Rev 4 and ends with the "last trump" Rev 11:15-19, spoken of in the 1 Thess 4:15-17 passage. The second extended vision or witness begins at Rev 12 and ends with the First Resurrection (Rev 20:1-6). Also, note the same event as recorded in Dan 12:1-3. Many of those who died during the Great Tribulation (A.D. 66-70) were raised to everlasting life, thus partaking of the First Resurrection. Those alive at the appearing of the Lord at the end of those last days of Israel would be caught up with the Lord to meet Him in the air, a thoroughly spiritual, yet real event that would enable them to walk with Christ in heavenly places shining brightly in Christ like the firmament while they yet lived on the earth, as Daniel had prophesied.

destruction comes upon them, as labor pains upon a pregnant woman. And they shall not escape. 4 But you, brethren, are not in darkness, so that this Day should overtake you as a thief. 5 You are all sons of light and sons of the day. We are not of the night nor of darkness. 6 Therefore let us not sleep, as others do, but let us watch and be sober. 7 For those who sleep, sleep at night, and those who get drunk are drunk at night. 8 But let us who are of the day be sober, putting on the breastplate of faith and love, and as a helmet the hope of salvation. 9 For God did not appoint us to wrath, but to obtain salvation through our Lord Jesus Christ, 10 who died for us, that whether we wake or sleep, we should live together with Him. 11 Therefore comfort each other and edify one another, just as you also are doing.

One notes in the continuation of the narrative from 1 Thess 4 that the "Day" of the Lord is upon the first century church and that these Thessalonian Christians were to be sober, alert, and knowledgeable of what was about to happen in the world so as to be saved from the judgment that was imminent.

The judgment upon Jerusalem and the Roman Empire, for that matter, was sudden and severe as the capstone of the Days of Vengeance spoken of in Luke.[284] The Day of the Lord was the wrath of God upon those who had killed the prophets from righteous Abel to Jesus. This 1 Thess 4-5 passage is not speaking of a secret rapture of the church, but is about the coming of the Lord and His Kingdom, a spiritual and indeed enigmatic and mysterious event having occurred during the first century as clearly evidenced by the prophecy-fulfilling event that occurred in A.D. 70, Christ's appearing, His Parousia. One can deduce that the Lord was about to come in salvation and judgment. He would cause those saints who died in Him to rise (the First Resurrection) and would change those who were alive and remaining unto His coming in A.D. 70. The Apostle Paul was preparing the churches for the great and terrible Day of the Lord by exhorting the church to comfort one another with those words. The Apostle Peter spoke similar words of encouragement to the dispersed converted

---

[284] Luke 21:21-23.

Jewish congregations when these saints were under unbearable persecution and thought that the Lord was delaying His coming to their detriment.[285]

The Two Witnesses in the Revelation of Jesus Christ Partook of the First Resurrection

Another passage of Scripture that is established in the Resurrection of Christ and which culminates in the First Resurrection and the resuscitation of the Church is St. John's vision of the two witnesses in Rev 11.[286] This passage is very much like the prophet Zechariah's vision of lampstands and olive trees used to inspire and pastorally motivate the Jewish exiles to rebuild the second temple and to let nothing stop them for, as God spoke to Zechariah, this work would be accomplished successfully by the Spirit of God.[287] In a similar manner, in the Revelation of Jesus Christ, at the end of the Revelation's first major vision, the Holy Spirit-filled Church is depicted as arrayed in sackcloth while ministering the Last Days prophetic message to doomed Jerusalem during the 42 months of the Great Tribulation. The Church here in the Rev 11 passage is presented as two witnesses symbolizing the preaching of the Gospel of Jesus the Christ from both the Law and the Prophets. We see the Church preaching and praying like the prophets of the Old Testament who, like Elijah, could open or close heaven's rains with their prayers and could speak to mountains of impedance to be removed, as Christ taught her to do.[288] As a result of her preaching and manner of living under the reigning King of kings, she was persecuted and nearly snuffed from existence

---

[285] 2 Pet 3. Note again, there is no section break between vs. 13 and vs. 14 in 2 Pet 3, which lets the reader and hearer know that Peter's first century audience of converted Jews were looking forward to the immanent Coming of the Lord (as a thief in the night), the Day of the Lord, the end of the Last Days, the inauguration of the New Heavens and New Earth, and the time when the old heavens and earth would melt away with fervent heat. This is symbolic language pertaining to the burning down and away of Jerusalem, its temple, and its Old Covenant redemptive sacraments forever.

[286] Rev 11; Matt 5:17-19.

[287] Zech 4.

[288] C.f., Jas 5:15-17; Matt 17:20; 21:21.

by her persecutors, who filled with contempt for her and, having no decency, refused to bury the dead bodies of her martyred members. The grand surprise to the world was the coming of the Church's Chief Shepard: His Parousia. At Christ's coming He raised and resuscitated His persecuted Church. The act of the Church being caught up to meet her coming Lord in A.D. 70, was written in the Latin Vulgate as *rapio* for the two words "caught up" used in 1 Thessalonians 4:17. In this author's opinion, this is what the rapture really was as opposed to a future escape from a future tribulation. The Church's martyrs partook of the First Resurrection, and those alive at His coming were raised and seated with Christ in heavenly places to forever be with Him as they continued their lives after A.D. 70. The differences after A.D. 70, were that the Church's primary *thorn in the flesh* and persecutor, apostate Jerusalem, was gone forever, and that the Church shined brightly for the world to see her Lord and her good works, which were salvific to the world and resulted in the rapid and powerful spread of Christianity in the world from the end of the first century onward to today.

The Church Made Herself Ready for the First Century Marriage Supper of the Lamb

In A.D. 70, with apostate Jerusalem gone, and the beginning of the end of the Roman Empire inaugurated, Satan bound and in the abyss, and the Church (the New Jerusalem) free from her enemies, the coast was now clear to continue Christ's offensive push to grow His Church and Kingdom. The nations were to be discipled to praise, obey, and sup with the King in the Holy Eucharist, or Lord's Supper. The Bride of Christ, the Church, had made herself ready. The Church, made up of those converted from among the Jews and the Gentiles, who would now exist as one holy, covenant people in Christ Jesus,[289] would now become betrothed to her Lord during that first century Parousia.[290] This Marriage Supper of the Lamb was not and is not a future event. On the contrary, it was a covenantal event that occurred in A.D. 70, for the first time as Jesus had promised

---

[289] Gal 3:27-29.

[290] Rev 19:6-8.

His disciples. The time had come for Jesus to eat and drink with His New covenant people, the Church, in His Father's Kingdom. Recall Jesus' words to His disciples, "But I say to you, I will not drink of this fruit of the vine from now on until that day when I drink it new with you in My Father's kingdom.[291] The time had come for the Marriage Supper of the Lamb, the Eucharist, the Lord's Supper. As St. John revealed in the Revelation of Jesus Christ:

> "After these things I heard a loud voice of a great multitude in heaven, saying, "Alleluia! Salvation and glory and honor and power belong to the Lord our God! For true and righteous are His judgments, because He has judged the great harlot who corrupted the earth with her fornication; and He has avenged on her the blood of His servants shed by her." Again they said, "Alleluia! Her smoke rises up forever and ever!" And the twenty-four elders and the four living creatures fell down and worshiped God who sat on the throne, saying, "Amen! Alleluia!" Then a voice came from the throne, saying, "Praise our God, all you His servants and those who fear Him, both small and great!" And I heard, as it were, the voice of a great multitude, as the sound of many waters and as the sound of mighty thunderings, saying, "Alleluia! For the Lord God Omnipotent reigns! Let us be glad and rejoice and give Him glory, for the marriage of the Lamb has come, and His wife has made herself ready." And to her it was granted to be arrayed in fine linen, clean and bright, for the fine linen is the righteous acts of the saints. Then he said to me, "Write: 'Blessed are those who are called to the marriage supper of the Lamb!' " And he said to me, "These are the true sayings of God."[292]

And through the Church, the whole world is now called to this Marriage Supper of the Lamb called the Communion of Saints, and more specifically the

---

[291] Matt 26:29.

[292] Rev 19:1-9.

Eucharist, the feast of the living Lamb of God who gave Himself for the sins of the world.

The Messages of Faith and Perseverance to the Saints from the Epistle to the Hebrews and the Revelation of Jesus Christ

Now that most of the components of the Last Days and Christ's Parousia have been addressed, I'd like to place into the historical and eschatological context two New Testament books that were written, distributed, and read to prepare the Church for the horrendous, yet glory-bound time of the Great Tribulation: The Epistle to the Hebrews and the Revelation of Jesus Christ. When reading these inspired works within the context of redemptive history, one begins to understand why John the Baptist, Jesus, and the apostles spoke of God's immanent wrath to come upon Jerusalem and why the city would be left as desolate due the people's rejection of Him. These help to answer the question as to why St. John said in his time that "it is the last hour."[293] This brief section aligns the first century eschatological events associated with Christ's Parousia to what the authors of Hebrews and the Revelation had to say. Why just these portions of Sacred Scripture? To be sure, these two works were written during the first century when the heat of the Great Tribulation was about to break forth. It was time for the churches to exercise perseverance, that virtuous fruit of the Spirit, until the end of the Great Tribulation.[294] Her members would be required to hold fast to the faith while enduring fiery trials of loss of goods, imprisonment for the faith, being ostracized from family and society, and having to watch the same trials being endured by their pastors, bishops, and apostles. The Spirit of God also gives us today lessons from Hebrews and the Revelation so that we may carry on the overcoming victory and virtues of prudence, justice, patience, perseverance, courage, self-control and fervent love modeled by the first century Church as Jesus currently builds His kingdom and Church.

---

[293] 1 John 2:18

[294] Dan 12:11-12; Matt 10:22; 24:13.

The writer of the Epistle to the Hebrews commended the Church as she persevered through hardships of the plundering of her goods for the testimony of Jesus Christ, especially during those last days. The Christians had to maintain their faith and patience so that they could inherit the promise of a New Heavens and New Earth and life in the Thousand-Year Reign of Christ.[295] This exhortation to persevere and to exercise faith and patience preached by the Lord's apostles, prophets, evangelists, pastors, and teachers spurred the church on to good works and her overcoming sin and any bitterness or hatred of others arising from their persecution. The Christians were not to allow their love to wax cold due to lawlessness. Jesus and His apostles exhorted them to persevere and to love not their lives unto death. As St. Paul said, these things were written for those first century Christians as an admonition for those upon whom the end of the ages "had come."[296]

Although we today will not see another "last days," as defined in Scripture, or a Great Tribulation that ends with the destruction of the Old Covenant world, we today do pray for grace to persevere in the faith as did our first century Christian brethren so that we hold fast until death, until that day when we see Christ face to face. There will indeed be a day when we physically die, if we are not of that generation that sees the expiration of the Thousand-Year Reign. In addition, there will be a day when our Lord Jesus, according to the Catholic Church's creeds and Catechism, returns to judge the living and the dead. We, therefore, want to live in a way pleasing to Christ Jesus in every thought, word, and deed.

In Hebrews, a message of separation and perseverance was targeted toward the converted Jews along with an exhortation to come out from among their unbelieving Jewish brethren who rejected their Messiah. They were to bear Christ Jesus' reproach, even if it meant loss of goods, or ostracism from family and Jewish society. St. Paul, the likely writer of this epistle warned his audience that there was no continuing earthly Jerusalem for the Jews and that there was no other salvation or redemption from sin if Christ Jesus were publicly rejected. The notion of separation from faithless Jerusalem before its destruction was a

---

[295] Heb 6:11-12.

[296] 1 Cor 10:11; Heb 9:26.

central theme in Hebrews as well as in the Revelation of Jesus Christ, in which St. John exhorted them to come out from Jerusalem, or Babylon, and to be separate.

The Epistle to the Hebrews immediately lays the foundation that God in those last days had spoke to the Hebrews through Jesus, the exalted Son of God, who was attested to by signs and wonders. Christ is presented as above all creation and as seated at God's right hand until all his enemies are made a footstool for His feet. The Hebrews are encouraged with the words that Christ Jesus is the destroyer of death and of eternal bondage to death, as well as that Prophet of God who was to come and save them. Christ is the promiser of eternal rest, the compassionate High Priest after the Order of Melchizedek, and the Mediator of the New Covenant. The Hebrews were exhorted about the eternal dangers of turning away from Christ and going back to a Pharisaical Judaism and its redemptive animal sacrifices. They were reminded that Jesus' once-and-for-all sacrifice was the only sacrificial offering acceptable to God for the perfection of the saints. Apart from reliance on the blood sacrifice of the Son of God on the cross, there would be no hope for salvation. Further, after the destruction of the temple, there was no longer a priest-offered sin-atoning sacrifice in Jerusalem, and if there were ever an attempt at such, it would have been an abomination before God. The Apostle Paul in Heb 11 reminds the Hebrews of the faith of their forefathers and foremothers in the Christ to come, and how that those who had gone before had died persevering in the faith, anchored in the hope of Jesus and His coming salvation and that of the Kingdom of God. It would be through the prayerful exercise of faith and perseverance that the Hebrews would inherit the Kingdom of God at the end of the Great Tribulation. Finally, St. Paul exhorted his Hebrew brethren that they should not turn back to perdition and to those things that were but a type and shadow of Christ and the Kingdom to come because the Christians were about to receive an unshakable kingdom and an eternal city. They were to hold onto the hope of God's making all things new at the end of the Great Tribulation, as they were about to see the coming Mount Zion. They were about to be a part of the city of the living God, the heavenly Jerusalem. Paul wrote that the converted Hebrews had come to "an innumerable company of angels, to the general assembly and church of the firstborn who are registered in heaven, to God the Judge of all, to the spirits of just men made perfect, to Jesus the Mediator of the new covenant, and to the blood of sprinkling that speaks better things than that of Abel." He added under the inspiration of the Holy Spirit, "...since we are receiving a kingdom which cannot be shaken, let us have grace, by which we may serve God acceptably with reverence and godly fear. For our God is a consuming fire."[297]

His stern warning would keep the Hebrews cleaving in faith to God through Christ:

> "See that you do not refuse Him who speaks. For if they did not escape who refused Him who spoke on earth, much more shall we not escape if we turn away from Him who speaks from heaven, whose voice then shook the earth; but now He has promised, saying, "Yet once more I shake not only the earth, but also heaven." Now this, "Yet once more," indicates the removal of those things that are being shaken, as of things that are made, that the things which cannot be shaken may remain;"[298] and, "Therefore, brethren, having boldness to enter the Holiest by the blood of Jesus, by a new and living way which He consecrated for us, through the veil, that is, His flesh, and having a High Priest over the house of God, let us draw near with a true heart in full assurance of faith, having our hearts sprinkled from an evil conscience and our bodies washed with pure water. Let us hold fast the confession of our hope without wavering, for He who promised is faithful. And let us consider one another in order to stir up love and good works, not forsaking the assembling of ourselves together, as is the manner of some, but exhorting one another, and so much the more as you see the Day approaching.[299]

---

[297] Heb 12:22-29.

[298] Heb 12:25-27.

[299] Heb 10:19-25.

Like the Epistle to the Hebrews, the Revelation of Jesus Christ, written by St. John (*c.* A.D. 65-66, from the Isle of Patmos), also communicated a first century last day's message of encouragement and warning to the Seven Churches of Asia Minor. Caesar Nero had banished St. John there for his testimony of Jesus and the Word of God. Christ's coming was immanent, and the end of the Old Covenant age was at hand. The Revelation of Jesus Christ revealed to the Church a King reigning in heaven who saw their plight and was ready to bring their deliverance as well as a severe judgment to their enemies. The Revelation begins by revealing Christ as a victorious conqueror riding on a white horse to save His people and to bring justified punishment upon their persecutors. This revelation was meant to root and ground Christ's Church, as she that was sorely persecuted and nearly crushed to the ground.[300]

The Revelation depicts the city of Jerusalem as still standing along with its temple, with Caesar Nero on the throne and demonic forces raging. They were causing havoc throughout the Roman Empire with wars, rumors of wars, and destruction. Satan had been thrown down to earth along with a third of the rebellious angels prior to the 3 ½ years of the Great Tribulation that were about to begin.[301] The demonic hosts were targeting those loyal to Jesus Christ for death. The specifically targeted seven churches of Asia Minor (modern-day Turkey) in Rev Chapters 2-3, were located in cities where emperor-worshipping

---

[300] Matt 24:22; Rom 9:28; 1 Pet 4:12.

[301] An elaboration regarding Satan's history and status is in order here. Church tradition teaches that the angel Satan fell from grace at some time prior to the creation of man. This fallen angel was subsequently cast out of the highest heaven where God is seated. Isaiah 14:12 is a foundational passage used to refer to Satan, or Lucifer, as the king of Babylon was also referred to and called in this Isaiah passage. Satan is then presented again in the opening chapter of the book of Job as wandering throughout the earth as the accuser, or adversary, whose motive is to thwart God's plans and accuse mankind of punishable sins. As redemptive history nears the birth of Christ Jesus, St. John in Rev 12 presents Satan symbolically as a dragon seeking to destroy the Christ and His people. Finally, as we near the end of the Last Days of the Great Tribulation, St. John records the battle in the heavens between St. Michael the Archangel and his angels and Satan and his angels. Finally, in Rev 12:9-17, one reads that Satan and his angels were cast out of the heavens and thrown to the earth. Satan's anger and wicked works against Christ and His Church were intensified as a result for he knew that his time was short, only three-and-a-half-years until Christ ends the Great Tribulation with His Parousia and with his being bound to no longer deceive the nations.

cults, heretics teaching false doctrines, and demon-infiltrated Jewish synagogues resided.[302] Jesus referred to these synagogues as synagogues of Satan because they were persecuting the churches and causing the disciples of Jesus either to be murdered for their Christian testimony, or to stumble away from the faith altogether. This revelation was given to St. John prior to the Great Tribulation to reveal to the Church their Messiah as the King of the universe, as the Lord of the Church and the One in authority and in control, and as the only One worthy to open the New Covenant scroll and inaugurate the coming of the Kingdom of God in power.

There are many themes contained in the Revelation's epistolary section (Rev 1-3); its first vision (Rev 4-11); its second vision (a second testimony in Rev 12-20); and in its vision of the New Heavens, New Earth, and the New Jerusalem after the Great Tribulation (Rev 21-22). The first theme was the time is at hand. Written perhaps one to two years prior to the Great Tribulation, the Revelation presents what would shortly take place upon Jerusalem and the Roman Empire as a whole. Jerusalem is symbolized in the Revelation as Babylon the Harlot, the False Prophet, Egypt, and Sodom. The Roman Empire is symbolized as the Beast from the Sea and as the Dragon. "The time is at hand," was a message that prepared the Church for the Lord's immanent appearing and the coming of the Kingdom. Secondly, the theme of days of vengeance[303] depicts God's sending destructive plagues, wars, and conflagrations as just judgments that occurred within the opening of the seven seals (Rev 6-8) and the blowing of the seven trumpets (Rev 8-11). Similar to this first vision that includes both seals and trumpets, the second vision (a second witness) contains seven chalices that pour out the wrath of God (Rev 15-16). With those judgments came the end of the days of Old Covenant Israel in which the blood of the prophets was avenged on that "terminal" generation who was alive between A.D. 30 and A.D. 70.[304]

There is another theme associated with the Lord Jesus' immanent return and very near to St. John's epistle, in which he writes to the Church, "It is the last

---

[302] Rev 2:9; 3:9.

[303] Luke 21:22.

[304] Matt 11:16; 12:34-42, 45; 23:36; 24:34.

hour."[305] The theme, "I come quickly," meant exactly that. St. Peter told his first century listeners that they were about to experience this coming and that they should be diligent to be found by Him in peace, without spot and blameless.[306] Finally, the theme that the Lord Jesus reigns is clearly portrayed in these visions of the Lord Jesus, which would have given great comfort to the saints as the Old Covenant world, and the whole Roman world for that matter, was collapsing around them. Jesus was the King ruling all things from heaven. The Lord's people were affirmed in the truth that the Lord saw and knew their hardships along with their being cast out of their synagogues, communities, and Jerusalem. The Revelation of Jesus Christ affirmed Christ's people in the truth that their enemies' coming defeat as well as the Church's salvation was at hand. They were to stand fast and overcome, for the reward would be reserved for the overcomer.[307]

---

[305] 1 John 2:18.

[306] 2 Pet 3:14-15.

[307] Rev 2:7, 11, 17, 26-29; 3:5, 12, 21.

TABLE 5. FROM THE INAUGURATED KINGDOM TO THE KINGDOM'S FINAL CONSUMMATION.

Since the Lord's Parousia at the end of the first century, Christ, by the Spirit of God has progressively gone forth, offering salvation to whosoever would believe the Gospel of the Kingdom of God. Christ Jesus has offered and continues to offer terms of unconditional surrender to the entire world in every age. He and His Church will neither fail nor be discouraged until He has established justice in the earth. The coastlands shall await His law.[308]

In our presentation of *Chronological Timeline 6*, we will expound upon what we can know pertaining to the truths of the New Heavens and New Earth and the Thousand-Year Reign of Christ the King. We will also look at what happens at the expiration of the current Thousand-Year Reign of Jesus Christ. Finally, we will address those events anticipated to occur during the final judgment of the living and the dead.

The Kingdoms of this World Have Become the Kingdoms of Our Lord and of His Christ

The prophesies of Daniel and St. John in the Revelation of Jesus Christ align at essentially the same points, namely the end of the age, the destruction of Jerusalem and the Old Covenant, and the coming of the Kingdom of God. Daniel prophesied about our Lord's coming after the first century Great Tribulation and how it would be the time when the saints would possess the Kingdom of God Most High. Daniel, however, wanted to know more about the beast of Rome and how this transfer of the Kingdom would come about. Daniel

---

[308] Isa 42:4.

Chapter 7 elaborates upon the events leading up to point where the saints would possess the kingdom.[309]

> "But the saints of the Most High shall receive the kingdom, and possess the kingdom forever, even forever and ever…"I was watching; and the same horn [interpreted as Emperor Nero] was making war against the saints, and prevailing against them, until the Ancient of Days came [the Parousia of our Lord Jesus Christ], and a judgment was made in favor of the saints of the Most High [the Judgment of the Day of the Lord as prophesied by Jesus], and the time came for the saints to possess the kingdom [the reward of the perseverance of the saints who were martyred and those who were alive at His coming, His Parousia]. "Thus he said: 'The fourth beast shall be a fourth kingdom on earth (the Roman Empire), which shall be different from all other kingdoms, and shall devour the whole earth, trample it and break it in pieces. The ten horns are ten kings who shall arise from this kingdom [according to Ferrar, F.W., the kings of 10 imperial provinces: Italy, Achaia, Asia, Syria, Egypt, Africa, Spain, Gaul, Britain, and Germany].[310] And another shall rise after them [Emperor Nero]; he shall be different from the first ones, and shall subdue three kings. He shall speak pompous words against the Most High, shall persecute the saints of the Most High, and shall intend to change times and law. Then the saints shall be given into his hand for a time and times and half a time [depicting the severe distress and persecution of the church during the 3 ½ year Great Tribulation, A.D. 66-70]. 'But the court shall be seated,[311] and they shall take away his dominion, to consume and destroy it forever [Caesar Nero eventually committed suicide

---

[309] Dan 7:18, 21-27.

[310] Ferrar, F.W., The Early Days of Christianity. 1882, p. 532.

[311] Ps 149:5-9.

and the subsequent emperors were executed and their rule ceased]. Then the kingdom and dominion, and the greatness of the kingdoms under the whole heaven, shall be given to the people, the saints of the Most High. His kingdom is an everlasting kingdom, and all dominions shall serve and obey Him.'

Daniel's passage here depicts the struggles leading up to the coming of the Kingdom of God in A.D. 70, and the reward for the living and martyred saints who would receive that Kingdom. Christ is the one who definitively brought His Kingdom and His saints with Him to judge the kings of the earth. From that first century on, Christ has continued reigning and conquering as King of all kings and Lord of all lords. We will see the fruits of His Kingdom progressively realized on earth in time just as we have seen the earth greatly Christianized since Christ's first century Parousia.

In the Revelation of Jesus Christ, we read at the end of the first extended vision in Revelation after the Seventh Trumpet is blown,

> "Then the seventh angel sounded: And there were loud voices in heaven, saying, "The kingdoms of this world have become the kingdoms of our Lord and of His Christ, and He shall reign forever and ever!" And the twenty-four elders who sat before God on their thrones fell on their faces and worshiped God, saying: "We give You thanks, O Lord God Almighty, the One who is and who was and who is to come, because You have taken Your great power and reigned. The nations were angry, and Your wrath has come, and the time of the dead, that they should be judged, and that You should reward Your servants the prophets and the saints, and those who fear Your name, small and great, and should destroy those who destroy the earth." Then the temple of God was opened in heaven, and the ark of His covenant was seen in His temple. And there were lightnings, noises, thunderings, an earthquake, and great hail.[312]

---

[312] Rev 11:15-19.

Table 5. Christ's Kingdom Continues to Fill the Earth Until the Kingdom's Final Consummation

The Current 1000-year Reign of Christ (1000 to be taken figuratively, not literally)
The Inaugurated New Heavens and Earth
Mount Zion's progressive filling of the Earth

Chronological Timeline

A.D. 70 ● —————————————————————————————— ● **A.D. ???**

Isa 42:4 He will not fail or be discouraged till he has established justice in the earth; and the coastlands wait for his law.

Christ's Dominion Fills the Earth in Every Realm

1 Cor 15: 24Then comes the end, when he delivers the kingdom to God the Father after destroying every rule and every authority and power. 25For he must reign until he has put all his enemies under his feet. 26The last enemy to be destroyed is death. 27"For God[c] has put all things in subjection under his feet." ...28When all things are subjected to him, then the Son himself will also be subjected to him who put all things under him, that God may be all in all.

When our Lord Returns at the end of this kingdom age to judge the living and the dead, then the Kingdom of God will be consummated, redemption is accomplished, and the meek inherit the earth.
Time is no more, and the saints are forever with their God
The tabernacle of God continues with men who then will experience the consummated New Heavens and New Earth

Nicene Creed: "He (Jesus) will come again in glory to judge the living and the dead and his kingdom will have no end."

Impacts of the Current Reign of Jesus Christ, the King of the Kingdom of God (in time and on earth)
(Symbolic and literal realities by grace through faith...BELIEVE and EMBRACE THEM)
Isa 2, 65; Ezek 40-48; Mic 4; Zec. 14; Ps(s) 1, 2, 110; Isa 65:17-66:24.

- The Kingdom of God and the Church shall be blessed, exalted, and the nations shall flow into it
- People from every nation will come to worship the King in His Church, Zion, the New Jerusalem
- The Law of God with its Life-giving instructions and grace will flow from the Church to the nations
- The Church will be vibrant and growing as her priests disciple the nations in the commands of Christ
- Nations shall humble themselves to Christ and His laws
- Nations will serve the Lord with fear, while rejoicing with trembling, and paying homage to Christ
- The former Old Testament order/heavens and earth shall not come to mind; No more weeping.
- The Church, the New Jerusalem, shall be a joy and be visited with blessings
- Infants shall thrive; mankind will, generally speaking, have long lives of fruitfulness, blessing, and prosperity as a norm for Christians
- Every believing man shall have his property, prosperity, a fruitful wife, and blessed children
- The Church will be characterized by holiness unto the Lord, her people seated in heavenly places
- Sinners, certainly a minority group, shall be outside the Kingdom and the Church's gates
- Unbelieving and sinning nations, neglecting the Lord's worship shall be plagued and punished
- Christ's people shall dwell securely, enjoying their work, their production, and their prosperity
- Children shall come forth blessed in abundance for prosperity and heritage, and not for calamity
- God will hear His peoples' prayers and answer speedily
- Peace will grow among nations and within nature as Christ is obeyed as King of Kings
- Warfare shall fade away, and the Church shall dwell safely and be protected by rulers of nations
- Worship of the Lord God will be celebrated daily
- Symbolically, blessings will abound in the earth as though the deserts were blooming like a rose

After this Current Thousand Year Reign of Christ Expires: (Rev 20)

- Satan released from his prison/the abyss to deceive the nations
- Satan incites the unbelieving nations (symbolically called Gog and Magog) to attack the Church
- This short-lived and final contempt against Christ and His Church is vanquished quickly
- God's fire comes down from heaven
- God judges the devil and casts him into the Lake of Fire
- Christ comes forth to judge the living and dead and assembles the dead of all time to come before Him for judgment
- Those whose names are in the Book of Life escape this final judgment and punishment
- Christ judges all the dead according to their works
- Christ casts death and Hades into the Lake of Fire; this is the Second Death
- Those not found written in the Book of Life were thrown into the Lake of Fire

In this passage we see the definitive downfall of the enemies of Christ along with the First Resurrection of the just, all occurring as components of the A.D. 70 appearing of the Lord. We see the prophetic sign of the presence of Christ's appearing, represented as lightnings, noises, thunderings, and an earthquake, and great hail, the signs of which were very similar as the day God's wrath was placed upon Jesus Christ on the cross for the sins of mankind 40 years earlier. Recall the temporal resurrection of saints from the dead after Jesus had died on the cross, perhaps a precursor to the First Resurrection to come in A.D. 70.

> "From noon on, darkness came over the whole land until three in the afternoon. And about three o'clock Jesus cried with a loud voice, "Eli, Eli, lema sabachthani?" that is, "My God, my God, why have you forsaken me?" When some of the bystanders heard it, they said, "This man is calling for Elijah." At once one of them ran and got a sponge, filled it with sour wine, put it on a stick, and gave it to him to drink. But the others said, "Wait, let us see whether Elijah will come to save him." Then Jesus cried again with a loud voice and breathed his last. At that moment the curtain of the temple was torn in two, from top to bottom. The earth shook, and the rocks were split. The tombs also were opened, and many bodies of the saints who had fallen asleep were raised. After his resurrection they came out of the tombs and entered the holy city and appeared to many. Now when the centurion and those with him, who were keeping watch over Jesus, saw the earthquake and what took place, they were terrified and said, "Truly this man was God's Son!"[313]

The New Jerusalem was ushered in by the coming of Jesus the King, who is depicted in the Revelation as One riding on a White Horse. Contrary to dispensationalism's doctrine that the one riding the white horse of the Apocalypse is the Antichrist, Christ is actually the Conquering King in both "white horse"

---

[313] Matt 27:45-54.

depictions in the Revelation.[314] Furthermore, it was at this time the Lord Jesus bound Satan, placed him in the abyss, so that he could no longer deceive the nations with his lies, and the Word of the Lord could then go forth to the nations. Since then, bishops, priests, gospel preachers and teachers, and men and women young and old are thoroughly unfettered and unhindered to preach the Gospel of Kingdom and to say among the nations: "Our Lord reigns!" After the Parousia of Christ, the Kingdom began filling the earth and covering it as the waters cover the sea.

Today, the church of Jesus Christ has over 2 billion numbered faithful members who call Christ Jesus Lord of All and who seek to do the things that He has taught. In time and on earth, we can now expect to see what the prophets spoke, but did not get to experience. Humanity's worst and most troublesome days are behind, and mankind's best days are ahead in Christ Jesus. "Alleluia! For the Lord God Omnipotent reigns! Let us be glad and rejoice and give Him glory, for the marriage of the Lamb has come, and His wife has made herself ready." And to her it was granted to be arrayed in fine linen, clean and bright, for the fine linen is the righteous acts of the saints…And He has on His robe and on His thigh a name written: KING OF KINGS AND LORD OF LORDS.[315]

The Saints are Reigning with Christ Now During Christ's Current Thousand-Year Reign

With the Kingdom of God having come in power as Jesus prophesied, Christ's Thousand-Year Reign commenced. Since that Day of the Lord in A.D. 70, the Holy Trinity has been working mightily through Christ the King, who is directing and sustaining world leaders and world events, as well as the sacramental and preaching ministries of His Church by the Word of His power to the glory of His Father in Heaven. This is the biblical and rational reasoning to

---

[314] Rev 6:2 and 19:11 both depict Christ the King riding victoriously on a white horse. Even the saints coming with Him are riding white horses.

[315] Rev 19:6-8, 16.

say that the "last days" are behind us today, and the world's best days are ahead. The more we obey Christ's commands and abound in love while diligently with great love and care training our children and the nations to obey our Lord, the better these days and those ahead will be.

The Spirit of God is blowing where He wills, regenerating mankind, enabling him as vicegerent of Christ to see and to enter the Kingdom of God and then to sanctify and bless the earth. The Spirit is the essence of the New Covenant wherein regenerate mankind, by virtue of the new birth, has the Law of God written upon his heart and possesses a born-again spirit within himself that yearns to obey and honor Christ. Hearing and obeying the Lord, as Jesus taught, establishes one as blessed and as having built his life and heritage on a Rock, a solid foundation.[316]

The Father, through the works of the Son and the Holy Spirit, continues to bring all of Christ's enemies under His feet day by day until all of Christ's enemies are subdued. This implies that the world will be Christianized and filled with Christians, and that Christian nations will trust and love one another to the extent that they eventually will learn war no more, as Isaiah and Micah prophesied. Those who are in Christ Jesus now by faith are considered as reigning now with Him as He sits on His throne in heaven, and are seated with Him in heavenly places. They are priests and kings of God, a royal priesthood, a holy nation of Zion, the New Jerusalem, God's chosen people and special possession that shines as the noontime sun as the world sees their good works of faith, hope, and love.[317] And those saints who have passed from this life are reigning now in the heavenly kingdom, a living extension of the Kingdom of God on earth. They are the great cloud of witnesses praying for us, praising God and His Christ daily, and they will be His armies throughout time until the last day of this Thousand-Year age.

On earth, as the Kingdom of God is growing, there will be those people, tribes, tongues, and nations, who, although not regenerate or born again, will feign, or assume obedience to the King so as to function in the world peacefully

---

[316] Luke 6:47-48.

[317] 1 Pet 2:9, Matt 5:16.

and collaboratively.[318] These unregenerate yet perhaps agreeable folks who are assuming the mask of Christianity will be at risk of the final temptations to league with Satan at the end of the Thousand Years when he is released from the abyss and goes "out to deceive the nations which are in the four corners of the earth." Barring their repentance and obedience to Christ from the heart, which only a work of the Spirit of God can accomplish, those pretending obedience to Christ, but whose hearts are not pure before God, will be led to perdition. Those not obedient to Christ and who die prior to the end of the Thousand Years will die awaiting the final judgment of the Lord, the Second Death. St. John wrote, "Blessed and holy are those who share in the First Resurrection. The second death has no power over them, but they will be priests of God and of Christ and will reign with him for a thousand years."

The New Heavens and New Earth in Christ Have Already Been Inaugurated

With the coming of Christ's Kingdom, the inauguration, the definitive coming, of the New Heavens and New Earth in which righteousness dwells has commenced. This is what St. Peter spoke of to the converted Jews in his second letter when he said that after the old covenantal order is burned with fervent heat, they were to look patiently yet immediately for the New Heavens and New Earth that was about to come upon them.[319] Isaiah prophesied and provided the characteristic of this amazing event over 700 years earlier,

> "For behold, I create new heavens and a new earth; And the former shall not be remembered or come to mind. But be glad and rejoice forever in what I create; For behold, I create Jerusalem as a rejoicing, And her people a joy. I will rejoice in Jerusalem, And joy in My people; The voice of weeping shall no longer be heard in her, Nor the voice of crying. " No more shall

---

[318] See Ps(s) 81:15.

[319] 2 Pet 3:13.

an infant from there live but a few days, Nor an old man who has not fulfilled his days; For the child shall die one hundred years old, But the sinner being one hundred years old shall be accursed. They shall build houses and inhabit them; They shall plant vineyards and eat their fruit. They shall not build and another inhabit; They shall not plant and another eat; For as the days of a tree, so shall be the days of My people, And My elect shall long enjoy the work of their hands. They shall not labor in vain, Nor bring forth children for trouble; For they shall be the descendants of the blessed of the LORD, And their offspring with them. "It shall come to pass That before they call, I will answer; And while they are still speaking, I will hear. The wolf and the lamb shall feed together, The lion shall eat straw like the ox, And dust shall be the serpent's food. They shall not hurt nor destroy in all My holy mountain," Says the LORD.[320]

In time and on earth, incrementally, yet assuredly, these blessings of which Isaiah symbolically spoke will be realized as the Kingdom of God in this age. Christians will be blessed, dwell in prosperity and safety, and live long lives as the Lord wills. Eventually, even the animosity among the members of creation would be at peace and nations would lay down their weapons of war. Isaiah's vision of the New Heavens and New Earth to come is synonymous with his previous vision of the growth of the Kingdom of God in the earth.[321] We see in these prophesies a whole new world unfolding over time as Christians are fruitful in bearing and rearing a holy seed, godly children, who fill the earth and take part in every aspect of human life, including family, Church, State, and educational rulership.

We've spoken of progressive blessing, but what about suffering? To declare the truth of the New Heavens and New Earth and a growing Kingdom and Church, does not in any way imply that there will be no personal or collective suffering in this life or continuing requirement for one to take up one's cross and

---

[320] Isa 65: 17-25.

[321] Isa 2:1-4; c.f., Mic 4:1-13.

die to sinful self to follow the Lord, even to the extent of forsaking all of one's possessions if need be.[322] As the Kingdom of God continues to come in a world that loves itself and its secularism, we must remember the words of St. Paul, "We must through many tribulations enter the kingdom of God."[323] Sacred Scripture and the writings of the saints are replete with examples where God has required His people to suffer and encounter tribulation in this world for the purification, maturity, and salvation of His saints. Through tribulation, the saints have learned of God's love, faithfulness, and assured assistance to overcome sin, temptation, and the works of the evil one during severe times, including the Great Tribulation of the first century. Christ learned obedience through His earthly suffering and was able to aid and save others who were tempted as was He.[324] During the Great Tribulation, Jesus, as well as His apostles warned the heavily persecuted Church to bear up under trials (even if martyrdom was immanent), overcome sin, and persevere in the faith to obtain salvation.

> 1 Pet 1:6 In this you greatly rejoice, though now for a little while, if need be, you have been grieved by various trials, 7 that the genuineness of your faith, being much more precious than gold that perishes, though it is tested by fire, may be found to praise, honor, and glory at the revelation of Jesus Christ...

Jesus and St. Paul both sought to spare the Christians unnecessary suffering as the Great Tribulation neared and would conclude with Christ's Parousia. Speaking of those days of the Great Tribulation, Jesus said, "...woe to those who are pregnant and to those who are nursing babies in those days! And pray that your flight may not be in winter or on the Sabbath. St. Paul reiterated a similar warning to virgins regarding marrying. He didn't want them to suffer unbearably, especially with infants and young children; however, he did not forbid their marrying even though it would bring trouble and distress due to the near

---

[322] Luke 9:23; 14:27, 33.

[323] Acts 14:22.

[324] Heb 5:8; 2:18; 13:12.

coming of the Lord.[325] Sadly, this passage has been interpreted out of context by those who would reject being open to bearing children.

> "But this I say, brethren, the time *is* short, so that from now on even those who have wives should be as though they had none, those who weep as though they did not weep, those who rejoice as though they did not rejoice, those who buy as though they did not possess, and those who use this world as not misusing *it*. For the form of this world is passing away."[326]

With both blessings and the overcoming of suffering and tribulations, the conclusions of this book do, however, present the estate of a progressive Christianizing of the entire earth, its peoples, and all of its authorities, humbling themselves to Christ as King. As mentioned earlier, Jesus is Lord over the Church, heads of households (the domestic churches), the State, and all other rulers. Jesus Christ is head over each realm of authority in the earth. Yet, the Church plays a sanctifying and sacramental role in the realization of Christ's Kingdom in the earth due to being a steward and preacher of the Word of God to the world.

The New Heavens and New Earth are not new as to substance, but new as to *nature*. The New Heavens and New Earth are spiritual in nature, but have physical, material, and organizational manifestations, clearly visible to the world. The nature of the word "new" here is like that of every man who is in Christ being a "new" creation. That converted man still looks the same on the outside; however, the change that has occurred in his heart through Christ has vanquished original sin and is eradicating from the man the ongoing proclivity to yield to sin. He is new on the inside, and the manifestation is mighty and miraculous on the outside, perhaps even upon his physical appearance.

The outward manifestations of the New Heavens and New Earth since its first century inauguration are evident; for example, the fall of the Roman Empire, the Christianization of the same (now called Western Christian Culture), the Christianization of the world with nearly 2.4 billion professing Christians in

---

[325] Matt 24:19; 1 Cor 7:25-28.

[326] 1 Cor 7:29-31.

the earth, the progressive realization of peace throughout the world, the reduction and near annihilation of paganism, the building of Church edifices and cathedrals with spires pointing to God in nearly every country, and (within the Catholic Church) a diocese on every square mile of earth. Catholic, Orthodox, and Protestant churches are spreading throughout the earth declaring Jesus Christ is Savior, King, and Lord of all. We also see every tribe, tongue, and nation flowing into the church. It is always true that this growth has its ebbs and flows throughout history, but as Daniel truly saw, the little stone, the Kingdom of God, began in a small way, but it became and is becoming a great mountain covering the entire earth.

Jesus affirmed the manner in which the Kingdom grows, "To what shall we liken the kingdom of God? Or with what parable shall we picture it? It is like a mustard seed which, when it is sown on the ground, is smaller than all the seeds on earth; but when it is sown, it grows up and becomes greater than all herbs, and shoots out large branches, so that the birds of the air may nest under its shade." [327] Note as this New Heavens and New Earth spread over the globe, the peoples will find rest and peace in it. Further evidence of the progressive growth of the Kingdom of God all over the world is our noticing less warfare around the world than at any other time in history. History depicts a measurable reduction in the number of and intensity of wars and world wars. We see mankind's progressive and inevitable laying down weapons of warfare and seeking to cooperate and work with privately owned capital to build implements of production for the good of all. Problems and divisions in the Church, as well as problems in families and States due to sin and other elements, are and will be overcome in time in answer to Jesus' prayer that all His people "be one." This hope is an anchor to the soul as the Kingdom grows in time. We must be as patient with the Church and the Kingdom's growth as we are the spiritual growth of a newborn babe in Christ. Sanctification and purification take grace and time. As time rolls on, we will see oppressive governments and wicked rulers and administrations chastened by the One who sees from heaven and judges according to each one's works. This is why our Sovereign Lord tells us to fear not, for it is His good pleasure to give His people the Kingdom.

---

[327] Mark 4:30-32.

Today, we also see, as was seen in Ezekiel and Revelation, the Word of the Lord and the grace of the church's sacraments flowing from the church to the nations like a river for their healing. The Church now, out of much love, courageously and boldly reaches out to Jews, Muslims, pagans, and atheists alike to make them disciples of Christ so they can all become, as St. Paul said, the true Jews, Christians, who are circumcised in heart. We see Christ's Spirit within men of low-born to high-born estates, who bring Christianity and the Laws of Christ to their families, their governments, to all their works, and into every realm of public and private life, thus sanctifying the world and all of creation alike.

The prophet Jeremiah spoke of the blessing that would come with the Kingdom of God; "No more shall every man teach his neighbor, and every man his brother, saying, 'Know the Lord,' for they all shall know Me, from the least of them to the greatest of them, says the Lord. For I will forgive their iniquity, and their sin I will remember no more."[328] Since the fourth century, there have been Christian kings, Christian States, Christian political parties, and waves of Christian revivals throughout the world, especially after the grace of societal repentance after great sins or even after religious persecution had come to light. Even during times when the church was operating in a sinful manner, God raised up men and women, many of whom are now canonized saints, who would speak the truth to her sins, paving the way for God's gracious gift of repentance. Recall that one of Jesus' twelve disciples, Judas, was demon possessed and His ministry was not only not thwarted but also was ordained by God to be there and fulfill his role of betrayal. Technically, then, one twelfth of that seed of the church was demon-possessed. Yet, the Church overcame, thrived, and progressed according to the will of God and for His glory. The Spirit of God working through the Church has always confronted the foolishness, the sins, and the evils of the day to sanctify herself and the world as she worshipped and glorified God. Today, Zion speaks forth against the sins of pride, greed, wrath, envy, lust, gluttony, and sloth. She disciples the nations in the faith of Christ and His teachings and seeks to form her disciples in the virtues of chastity, temperance, charity, diligence,

---

[328] Jer 31:34.

patience, kindness, and humility, among other fruits of the Spirit.[329] Those who seek to control the earth, such as globalists, socialists, communists, secularists, and neo-pagans, will never prevail. Our Lord Jesus rules through His Church as her ministers speak out against the trafficking, mutilation, and abortion of children, along with confronting the propaganda of gender fluidity and other family-destroying tenets of this day. The Church's truth confronts the propaganda and myths of overpopulation, man-made climate change, the ever-wretched plagues of socialism and communism, the love of money in all its facets, as well as the sins and societal side effects of rejecting Jesus as Christ as Lord and Savior. None of these seeming impediments shall prevail against the living rivers of water of the Word of God that will flow from the Church in time and on earth.

Also encouraging, history is replete with great nations that sought to evangelize and disciple the nations of the world for Christ, such as the Carolingian Empire ruled by Charlemagne, the Christian King of Franks in the eighth century. Although he is known for his forcing his vanquished enemies to convert to Christianity, something the church ought not to have done since conversion is by the Spirit of God alone, this was nonetheless a clear example of a Christian ruler, perhaps with the best of intensions on behalf of their Lord, ruling his realm given his knowledge and opportunities at the time. Charlemagne was crowned King of the Holy Roman Empire in A.D. 800, by Pope Leo III.

History also points us to the Kingdom of God's coming in historical monarchical coronation rites, such as in the Primate's Prayer, in the 19th century's Hungarian Coronation Rite:

> *Almighty and everlasting God, Creator of all things, Commander of angels, King of kings, and Lord of lords, who caused your faithful servant Abraham to triumph over his enemies, gave many victories to Moses and Joshua, the leaders of your people, exalted your humble servant David to the eminence of kingship, enriched Solomon with the ineffable gits of wisdom and peace. Hear our humble prayers and multiply your blessings upon your servant,*

---

[329] Gal 5:19-26.

whom in prayerful devotion we consecrate our king; that he, being strengthened with the faith of Abraham, endowed with the meekness of Moses, armed with the courage of Joshua, exalted with the humility of David and distinguished with the wisdom of Solomon, may please you in all things and always walk without offense in the way of justice. May he nourish and teach, defend and instruct your Church and people and as a powerful king administer a vigorous regimen against all visible and invisible powers and, with your aid, restore their souls to the concord of true faith and peace; that, supported by the ready obedience and glorified by the due love of these, his people, he may by your mercy ascend to the position of his forefathers and, defended by the helmet of your protection, covered with your invincible shield and completely clothed with the heavenly armor, he may in total victoriously triumphs and by his [power] intimidate the unfaithful and bring peace to those who fight for you, through our Lord who by the vigor of his Cross has destroyed Hell, overcame the Devil, ascended into heaven, in whom subsists all power, kingship and victory, who is the glory of the humble and the life and salvation of his people, he who lives and reigns with you and the Holy Spirit forever and ever. Amen.

As the rite depicts, the Hungarians saw themselves as members of the one, holy, and Catholic Church, the Kingdom of God spreading across the face of the earth. The Hapsburg Dynasty's empire, including the nation of Hungary, at that time was wholly given to allegiance to the Holy Catholic Church, and that is why one can see some of the Church's liturgy within the coronation rite. Christ was acknowledged in these rites as far back as the 11th century.

Another example of the Kingdom of God's reference in State government is in 1665, at which time we saw the following act passed in reference to a biblical Christianity by the New York colonial legislature: "Whereas, The public worship of God is much discredited for want of painful [laborious] and able ministers to instruct the people in the true religion, it is ordered that a church shall be built in each parish, capable of holding two hundred persons; that ministers of every church shall preach every Sunday and pray for the king, queen, the Duke of York, and the royal family; and to marry persons after legal publication of license.' It was also enacted that 'Sunday is not to be profaned by travelling, by laborers, or vicious persons,' and 'church-wardens to report twice a year all misdemeanors, such as swearing, profaneness, Sabbath-breaking, drunkenness, fornication, adultery, and all such abominable sins." These were the laws of the colonies until 1683, which show the commitment the Crown and the colonies had to the Lord Jesus and to the Sacred Scripture. The legislatures saw that kings and all who were in authority, as well as their constituents, whether Christian or not, were humble to the laws of God as presented in the Sacred Scriptures. Jesus did command that the nations were to be discipled to obey His commandments. From these examples, one can clearly see that rulers of nations, provinces, tribes, and states can and should prudently legislate according to that which would please Christ. To not do so would lead the nations into chaos and ultimate destruction as happened to Egypt, Babylon, Persia, Greece, Rome, Sodom and Gomorrah, and apostate Jerusalem in A.D. 70.

Within these days of the growing New Heaven and Earth, it is the normal course of God's guiding, blessing, and sustaining the creation that children shall come forth blessed in abundance within families, especially Christian families, so that their offspring may continue to bless the earth in turn with a godly heritage. God ordained marriage between a man and woman making them one for the sake of a godly seed.[330] Godly children within a family are declared by God as the heritage of the righteous who will ensure a Christian culture. Children, the gift of God, should never be considered as a bothersome, unaffordable, or calamitous endeavor, as most of the world today sees children. A rich man once was recorded as saying to a Puritan godly man with many children in a meager estate, "Ah, these [children] are they which make a rich man poor." The godly father replied, "Nay, Sir, these are they which make a poor man rich." The Church fills with men, women, and children of every tribe, tongue, and nation, who come to the House of the Lord to partake of the New Covenant and feed upon the body and blood of the Lord Jesus Christ faithfully every Lord's Day in public worship. In time, one shall see an increasingly realized peace among nations and nature because of Jesus Christ being recognized, acknowledged, and obeyed as

---

[330] Mal 2:14-15.

King of Kings and Lord of Lords. This will inevitably result in warfare fading away, and the Church dwelling safely, protected by rulers of nations. Instead of seeing the earth progressively destroyed by the foolish lies of overpopulation and inevitable entropy, we will see a blessed abundance of resources among a growing godly population, not only through proliferation of intellect and technology, but also with the necessary blessing of God that causes the earth to abound. Instead of our thinking like unbelievers—that the pie that is the earth and its resources will be consumed and destroyed by a greater population—we need to speak and act like believers in the God who will make the pie bigger to accommodate more people. Prophetically speaking, the Kingdom of God's blessings are likened unto the deserts blooming like a rose by the power and blessing of God that will surely come to pass.[331] The exhortation from Zechariah to those of us alive today is not to despise the day of small beginnings when we see bits and pieces of godly progress in the world, for, as it is assuredly written, the Mountain of Lord's House will indeed fill the earth through faith and patience.

The Beautiful and Bountiful New Jerusalem, the Church, the Bride of the Lamb, Is Filling the New Heaven and New Earth

After our Lord saved His Church, bringing her through that Great Tribulation of the first century, St. John in the Revelation of Jesus Christ sees all tears being wiped away from the eyes of those who had lived in faith under the first heaven and first earth of Old Covenant Jerusalem and its temple.[332] This vision reminds one of the simultaneous sounds of great rejoicing and great weeping when the foundation of the re-built temple were laid during the days of Ezra the priest in 516 B.C.[333] The Jews rightly rejoiced to see the foundations of the new temple built, yet many of the older Jewish heads of households recalled the beauty of Solomon's temple, the old temple, a type of the old heavens and old earth to them, that was burned to the ground by King Nebuchadnezzar in

---

[331] Zech 4:6-10.

[332] Rev 21:1-8.

[333] Ezra 3:11-13.

586 B.C. Yet, the tears are wiped away in St. John's Revelation because the New Jerusalem transcends the old Jerusalem in every way. One of the seven angels shows St. John Zion, the great holy city of Jerusalem coming forth out of heaven, which depicts its origin. St. John's description of this vision is not intended to portray the science fiction of an entire city, or a large cathedral, literally coming down out of the sky and landing on earth, as if it were a large space platform. On the contrary, St. John is seeing the glorious church, the Bride of Christ, who, by virtue of the Spirit of God above, has made herself ready for the Marriage Supper of the Lamb, today's Eucharist, as the culmination of the Lord's Day liturgical worship. Recall Jesus telling His disciples that He would not drink the Eucharist, the Lord's Supper, with His disciples until He would drink it anew with His purified bride in the new kingdom, a time which came definitively at the coming of Christ's Kingdom in power.[334]

The beauty of the purified church is described symbolically as having "streets of gold, like transparent glass," depicting that which was purified, as the apostles decades earlier had spoken.[335] St. John affirms that he sees no physical temple in this symbolically portrayed city, a declaration that negates any significance whatsoever of a temple being rebuilt in the old Jerusalem in the Middle East, a teaching purported by dispensational literalists. The new dwelling place of God, on the contrary, is within men by the Spirit of God, as Jesus had spoken to the Samaritan woman.[336] St. John sees the Church filled with the redeemed from among all nations, including their kings, who bring their glory and honor into it.[337] This is the same glorious Church that continues to grow in these days of the 21st century as the Word of God goes forth into the world causing men to repent of their sin and to call upon His name. It should be mentioned that this Church existing now on earth, the Church Militant as it is called, is completely attached by spirit and covenant to the living saints who have passed from this life into the heavenly Kingdom. We say they are alive and among the great witnesses

---

[334] Matt 26:28-30.

[335] 2 Tim 2:14-26; 1 Cor 3:5-15; 1 Pet 1:6-8; 2 Pet 3:7; Rev 9:18.

[336] John 4:21-24.

[337] Rev 21:22-27.

of Christ in heaven praying for us. We, who are now alive in these days, are thus fellow partakers of that same First Resurrection by virtue of our baptism and are co-heirs of the heavenly Kingdom in Christ.

A timeless principle we learn about the Church from St. John comes from his warning to his first century brethren, which is appropriate for us to hear and heed today: "Blessed are those who do His commandments, that they may have the right to the Tree of Life, and may enter through the gates into the city. But outside [the Church and His Kingdom] are dogs and sorcerers and sexually immoral and murderers and idolaters, and whoever loves and practices a lie.[338] These things were written for our first century brethren's warning and admonition upon whom the ends of the ages had come, and they are now written for our admonition.[339] The Revelation of Jesus Christ was also written to encourage all of God's holy people from the first century on through to this present day and into the future. We, although not living in those last days, and although not having to go through a future Great Tribulation, must through the same faith and patience endure to the end in faith to enter God's rest, the eternal Sabbath, as those now seated in heavenly places in Christ Jesus.

The Kingdom is growing and its best days and ours are ahead. It is exciting to awaken every day knowing that Christ is King, His Kingdom and His Church are growing and filling the earth, we are alive in Christ and living under the watchful eye of our merciful God. The works of our hands will be blessed, our children will be fruitful and blessed, the devil is bound, and God's truth and justice are progressively and assuredly filling the earth. The mercies of God are new each day, and our Lord arises with healing in His wings daily. Therefore, we work, love, and build now, and we eagerly look forward to being with the King and His saints in the heavenly kingdom as we pass from this life, having been loyal to the King of the Kingdom. That is why we pray in faith believing we will receive the answers to the petitions, "Thy Kingdom come, Thy will be done on earth as it is in heaven."

---

[338] Rev 22:14-15.

[339] 1 Cor 10:11.

What Happens after This Thousand-Year Reign of Christ Expires?

When Christ's Thousand-Year Reign expires, which according to Scripture will occur when all of Christ's enemies have been made a footstool for Christ's feet and the entire world has tasted of the goodness of the Lord, Satan will be loosed from his holding place in the abyss and will work to deceive the nations to gather them against the Church one last time. St. John in Rev 12 applies the names attributed to the pagan nations found in Ezekiel 38:2 to represent symbolically the ungodly nations still remaining throughout the earth that would seek to put an end once and for all to the Kingdom of Christ and its inhabitants of Commandment-keepers on earth. Satan will inspire and gather the rebellious pawns from Gog and Magog "whose number is as the sand of the sea" (a reference to the covenant children of Abraham) together to battle. At that time, there will be no Great Tribulation as that which occurred in the first century, and the situation will not resemble Satan's first century war against the Child and the Woman as described symbolically in Rev 12. There is no indication within Sacred Scripture that there will be any significant amount of time at all in this last uprising, for as soon as this short rebellion begins, fire will come down from heaven and the devil will be cast into the Lake of Fire, where the kingdoms of Rome (the Beast and its Image Caesar Nero) and apostate Jerusalem (the False Prophet) will have been since A.D. 70. After this, the final judgment of the living and the dead will begin. At that time, the unbelievers and sinners will be raised on the last day of history at the conclusion of the Thousand Year Reign of Christ. They will be judged according to their works according to what had been written of them in *the books*.[340] They will subsequently be cast into the Lake of Fire, forever separated from God and His glorious Kingdom. Their names will not be found in the Book of Life. They will have never bowed the knee to the King Christ Jesus. Neither would they have acknowledged Christ's Lordship, nor obeyed His words or His teachings. Working lawlessness, they would hypocritically have feigned their Christianity and loyalty to the Lord for whatever reason, yet would not have

---

[340] Daniel, in Dan 7:10, and St. John in Rev 20:12 write of "the books" as being the records of the works of each member individually of mankind, by which they will be judged. Those whose names are written in the Book of Life, shall be saved on that last day of judgment, as written in Rev 20:15.

stored up treasure in heaven.[341] They will not be counted among those who took up their cross and followed Him. They would have loved their lives and sought to have saved themselves from the world's reproach; and, therefore, they would have horrifically lost their lives forever. Finally, after this eternal judgment, Death and Hades themselves will be cast into the Lake of Fire.

All of those remaining who had died in the faith prior to the expiration of the Thousand Years, as well as those in the faith who will be alive during that final coming of Christ, will be raised from the dead, as was Christ, and will assume their glorified bodies. Rev 20:11-15 gives us detail from which one can deduce that those in Christ who had passed from death to life through the new birth, the work of the Spirit of God, had also passed from eternal judgment because their names had been placed in the Book of Life from the foundations of the world. Another reference to the Book of Life was apparent when Jesus had said to His disciples who were glad the demons were subject to them, "...do not rejoice in this, that the spirits are subject to you, but rather rejoice because your names are written in heaven."[342] St. Paul considered his fellow workers in the gospel as having their names in the Book of Life.[343] St. John spoke the most about the Book of Life saying that those faithful followers of Christ who would overcome sin while undergoing temptation would NOT have their names blotted out from the Book of Life.[344]

There are other biblical references to the Book of Life. The followers of first century antichrist Nero and those who marveled at the strength of Rome over Christ Jesus would not have their names written in the Book of Life.[345] Only those whose names are in the Book of Life will enter the great city, the holy Jerusalem, that great and high mountain of Zion whose origin is out of heaven

---

[341] Matt 7:21-23; Luke 6:46.

[342] Luke 10:20.

[343] Phil 4:3.

[344] Rev 3:5

[345] Rev 13:8; 17:8.

from God.[346] Finally, St. John gives a warning to all to not alter the Revelation of Jesus Christ, "For I testify to everyone who hears the words of the prophecy of this book: If anyone adds to these things, God will add to him the plagues that are written in this book; and if anyone takes away from the words of the book of this prophecy, God shall take away his part from the Book of Life, from the holy city, and from the things which are written in this book.[347]

So, how does one make their calling sure as to their name being in the Lamb's book of life? St. Peter tells us, "...by giving all diligence, [to] add to our faith virtue, to virtue knowledge, to knowledge self-control, to self-control perseverance, to perseverance godliness, to godliness brotherly kindness, and to brotherly kindness love. For if these things are ours and abound, we will be neither barren nor unfruitful in the knowledge of our Lord Jesus Christ. For he who lacks these things is short-sighted, even to blindness, and has forgotten that he was cleansed from his old sins. Therefore, we are even more diligent to make our call and election sure and steadfast, for if we do these things we will never stumble; for so an entrance will be supplied to us abundantly into the everlasting kingdom of our Lord and Savior Jesus Christ."[348]

The Final Consummation of the Kingdom of God

Someday in the future, after Christ has judged the living and the dead; after Satan and all those not written in the Lamb's Book of Life are thrown forever into the Lake of Fire; when indeed after Death and Hades are thrown into the Lake of Fire, then Christ the King will present the consummated and perfected Kingdom of God to His Father as an offering so that God may be all in all.[349] When will all of Christ's enemies be made His footstool? That could be a hundreds of years from now or thousands of years from now, or more. We do not have evidence that

---

[346] Rev 21:27.

[347] Rev 22:18-19.

[348] See 2 Pet 1:5-11.

[349] 1 Cor 15:23-25.

ensures that we are now living in the last days merely because there are geopolitical troubles here and there. Yet, many in the Church and outside of her have considered themselves that terminal generation that would not pass away until His Second Coming.

St. Paul's 1 Corinthians Chapter 15 passage of the end of all time, in this writer's opinion, speaks to the end of time after Christ's reign and after His final coming, the last resurrection, and the judgment of the living and the dead at the Kingdom's consummation:

"But each one [raised] in his own order: Christ the first fruits, afterward those who are Christ's at His coming. Then comes the end, when He delivers the kingdom to God the Father, when He puts an end to all rule and all authority and power. For He must reign till He has put all enemies under His feet. The last enemy that will be destroyed is death…Now when all things are made subject to Him, then the Son Himself will also be subject to Him who put all things under Him, that God may be all in all."[350]

The Sacred Scripture and the Deposit of Faith stewarded by the Church gives us great hope and a rational and biblical optimism for the future wherein the Lord reigns and the whole earth rejoices. These instructions continue to offer encouragement, hope, an optimism for the future, and a great assurance in our Lord's guidance of, protection over, and blessing upon our labors to fulfill the cultural mandate given by God. Affirming this are the words of Saint Athanasius, who said that Psalm 97 foretells a world-wide salvation and that peoples of all nations will believe in Christ:

> "The Lord reigns; Let the earth rejoice; Let the multitude of isles
> be glad! Clouds and darkness surround Him; Righteousness
> and justice are the foundation of His throne. A fire goes before
> Him and burns up His enemies round about. His lightnings
> light the world; The earth sees and trembles. The mountains
> melt like wax at the presence of the Lord, At the presence of the
> Lord of the whole earth. The heavens declare His righteousness,

---

[350] 1 Cor 15:23-28.

and all the peoples see His glory. Let all be put to shame who serve carved images, who boast of idols. Worship Him, all you gods. Zion hears and is glad, And the daughters of Judah rejoice because of Your judgments, O Lord. For You, Lord, are most high above all the earth; You are exalted far above all gods. You who love the Lord, hate evil! He preserves the souls of His saints; He delivers them out of the hand of the wicked. Light is sown for the righteous, and gladness for the upright in heart. Rejoice in the Lord, you righteous, and give thanks at the remembrance of His holy name. The Lord is king, let earth rejoice, let all the coastlands be glad. Cloud and darkness are his raiment, his throne, justice and right."[351]

---

[351] Psalm 97.

HOW SHALL WE NOW LIVE? WHAT SHALL WE DO?

St. Luke recorded St. Peter's sermon to an audience of Jews and Gentile God-fearers during the Feast of Pentecost in A.D. 30, which included powerful words regarding the signs of coming Jerusalem's doom and the assurance of God's making Jesus, whom they had crucified, both Lord and Christ. Having heard these words, the audience, who had been cut to the heart from the preaching of Peter's words from God said, "Men and brethren, what shall we do?" St. Peter said to them, "Repent, and let every one of you be baptized in the name of Jesus Christ for the remission of sins; and you shall receive the gift of the Holy Spirit."[352] The preaching of the Gospel of the Kingdom of God also pricks hearts now and causes those touched by the Spirit of God to say the same thing, "What shall we do, and how shall we now live?" Knowing that the last days are behind us, and that our best days are ahead of us, how does one now live victoriously, joyfully (even if called to suffer) as a Christian? What does one do?

The answer is that we live in the same manner that our brother Christians lived prior to the Lord's first century coming: as overcomers. We have a strong and broad Christian history built upon those saints who have worked the earth and subdued every realm of it for Christ up to these days. Aside from Jesus, no Christians of the past were without temptation and sin, but they relied on God's continual grace and built to the glory of God, and God blessed them. The same can be said of us saints today and of those coming after us. "If God is for us, who can be against us."[353] The life we now live, even though subject to temptations, sin, and suffering is a life in which we continue to fulfill God's cultural mandate.

So, now we look at that period in *Chronological Timeline 5* between Christ's Parousia and His coming again to judge the living and the dead, Christ's Thousand-Year Reign.

---

[352] Acts 2:36-38.

[353] Rom 8:31.

To discuss how we shall live, we must consider who we are and how we stand as victors in Christ regardless of trials, temptations, weaknesses, and sins. This is necessary so that we are not manipulated away from an understanding of our true estate in Christ. We are redeemed and have been given the salvation and healing of the nations that comes with the coming of Christ's kingdom. This applies to our personal lives, as well as to the lives of those in our families, neighborhoods, cities, states, and nations in every sphere of life. We, as Christians, baptized into the name of the Father, Son, and Holy Spirit, are kings and priests unto God, filled with the Spirit of God. We are equipped for every good work of faith, hope, and love. We are supported by the full array of the living heavenly host, who is on our side and who prays for us and our Church, whose angels see the face of the Heavenly Father daily. This innumerable number of the heavenly host, the living witnesses in heaven, ever lives to intercede for the Church and the Kingdom of God and Christ's victory in the earth. We are a royal priesthood who daily yields our bodies and our works to our God and King, walking in this life as seated in heavenly places in Christ, partakers of the New Covenant, which is the Law of God written on our hearts, ratified by Christ's blood, and endowed with the Spirit of God who works in us to will and to perform God's good pleasure. We are those who love the Word of God as given to us in the Bible, on which we meditate day and night, performing those words when we rise up, when we lie down, when we walk by the way, and as we exercise prudence, justice, fortitude, and temperance in all of our works and in all of our spheres of authority and influence. By doing good, we, as Christians, let our light, Christ Himself, so shine before men that they see our good works and worship our God in heaven. We are devout members of His one, holy catholic and apostolic Church with roots buried deeply downward and branches bearing fruit upward. Filled with the Spirit of God and power from on High, we speak boldly to our family, our friends, our neighbors, and the nations this good news of the Kingdom so that all realize they are created in the image of God, must repent of sin, abound in good works of love to God and mankind, and bow to the Lordship of Christ unconditionally. We must tell all to realize Christ's removal of Satan's veil of deception from their eyes. Christ's is an imperialistic kingdom offering unconditional surrender with great love. We count it a joy to suffer for the name and work of Jesus Christ, not fearing the words of unbelievers, no matter how powerful, nor their ostracism, no matter how painful. We do not fear death, but we encourage ourselves in our Lord's atoning sacrifice for our sins and the King's victorious reign as we continue to overcome sin and live as followers of Christ in every thought, word, and deed. We advance the interests of the Kingdom of God. And even if we were to sin while living as Christians, as all men do, we have an Advocate with the Father, Jesus Christ, the Righteous One. We have the ministry of reconciliation in the Church for absolution, confessing our sins to one another, to God Himself either alone or in the Church's liturgy, and to our priests ordained to bring absolution, so as to get back into the good fight of faith having been forgiven.[354] Knowing also that our Lord is not willing that anyone should perish eternally, it is critical that we know the King, pray to God for the Kingdom to come, honor the King by being zealous for good works and by bearing a good testimony of love to the world with confident joy saying among the nations, "Our Lord reigns!"

This final section of our book points specifically, although not exhaustively, to what is expected of the man, woman, and child in Christ in this life as they live, move, and have their beings under the Lordship of Christ during this, His Thousand-Year Reign. This is who we are as individual Christians and who we are as a Spirit-filled collective of Christ as a Church.

Believe in and Obey Jesus as Lord, Christ, and King, and Come to His Church

St. Paul said to those Christians living and worshipping in Rome that, to be eternally saved, one must confess publicly that Jesus is Lord and Christ, and to believe in his heart that God raised Jesus from the dead. Paul wanted all men to declare Jesus Christ as Lord.[355] The apostles warned everyone to believe in Jesus and be baptized in the name of the Father, Son, and Holy Spirit. These first century preachers of the Gospel of the Kingdom exhorted all men to be

---

[354] James 5:16.

[355] Rom 10:9-10.

confirmed in the faith and filled with the Spirit of God through the Church's Sacraments of baptism and confirmation respectively. No man lives as an island. All of mankind is to hear the Word of the Lord coming forth from Zion, the Church, and to respond by going to the House of the Lord to hear and learn of His ways. The Lord loves the blessed unity of His saints as they gather for public worship. When attending the public worship of God, one should determine within one's heart to worship God with all of one's heart, soul, mind and strength, and to love and be kind to all of one's neighbors, especially their Christian brethren as a good steward of the relationships God gives us in life. Through prayers, conversations, and Eucharistic Adoration with the Father, Son, and Holy Spirit, as well as with all the saints (living and in heaven) and holy angels, one should nurture and maintain this very real fellowship with the living God, Christ the King, and all of the saints both living and departed.

Our Lord Jesus is building His church, outside of which there is no ordinary means of salvation.[356] Believers are to gather with Christ's church for the public worship of God, which would include not forsaking participation in the Eucharist with the body of Christ. This was the exhortation to the Hebrews Christians as they were enduring the Great Tribulation.[357] They were also taught to remember those who have the rule over them—their bishops, pastors, and spiritual authorities and mentors—remembering their godly way of life and their shepherding and feeding of souls. It is important that one not allow life's trials, setbacks, discouragements, or even the Church's insensitivities to tempt one to forsake assembling every Lord's Day with Christ's people to worship God publicly.

---

[356] From the writings of Saint Cyprian of Carthage. This is a dogma in the Catholic Church and the Eastern Orthodox Church.

[357] Heb 10:25.

Pray in Faith That God's Kingdom Come in Your Life, Your Family's Lives, Your Church, Your Nation, and Your World

The apostles and saints have always taught us that the fervent and effectual prayers of those in Christ avail much, and that we are to always be ready to pray on behalf of others. We pray for the Kingdom's coming on earth as it is in heaven, as our Lord taught in the "Lord's Prayer." We pray without ceasing for all peoples and for all things, praying for all who are in authority in governments, in the church, heads of house, individuals, and anything else our good Lord places within our hearts. Our desire is that God's Word and His will be manifested on earth in every realm of life from those of mankind in the lowest of estates to those who are of the highest estates from every race, tribe, and nation doing from the heart on earth what is done in heaven.

Knowing about the Kingdom also enables one to pray knowledgeably, "Thy Kingdom come, Thy will be done on earth as it is in heaven." When we pray that prayer that our Lord taught His disciples to pray, the "Our Father," or the "Lord's Prayer," especially within the public worship of God, we are praying that the rule of God, which is always manifest in heaven, would be manifest on earth likewise. We pray this prayer in faith knowing that when Christ's Kingdom comes in any personal or public situation, devils, lawlessness, and death are either immediately, or most likely ultimately over time, vanquished, while light, truth, and love begins to prevail. That is why we as well as the assembled Church must pray this prayer with fervency and patience with hope and faith that God hears and will answer according to His good pleasure. The answers that come may not be spiritual only, but may have real impacts on earth in our lives, our families, our nations, and our Churches. We pray this prayer knowing that the gates of hell shall not prevail against the advance of the Church and his Kingdom in all the earth. One's faith, hope, and acts of love are bolstered with great optimism when we pray "Thy Kingdom come."

Bear Hardship and Frustration as a Good Soldier of Christ the King

Realizing that the Kingdom of God is growing and filling the earth progressively, one must be prepared to recognize and endure the ebbs and flows of Kingdom growth, as well as the vexing nature of seeming defeats. The Church while obeying Christ and working to build in this world will many times experience, what the Book of Ecclesiastes calls frustration, or vexation, translated as "vanity." I would like to summarize some primary principles I've learned from the Book of Ecclesiastes because these truths have always taught the covenant people how to cope with and resolve the frustrations of life under the sun, this side of heaven, while God builds His Kingdom.

Eat, Drink, and Be Merry

In life, there is nothing better that a man should do than to eat his food with joy, drink good wine, and cause himself to see good in his work. This is the gift of God to a man as he lives his life before an all-seeing, all-knowing, and all-powerful God. This is God's blessed portion to the godly man.[358] The joy in one's labors will accompany him during the days of his life under the sun as the Lord builds His Church and His Kingdom.

Find Joy in a Spouse, Children, and in All Things

Realize that is it God's gift to find joy in every aspect of one's life and to enjoy living in general. Find joy in the wife of your youth and, as a result, find joy in all the children God would give to you. Wives and children are not a "ball and chain" to a man as the secularists say. On the contrary, marriage, as Peter Laffin has written, is a way "…to give [one's] all to something higher than [one's self],

---

[358] C.f. Ps(s) 1; 128; 103.

because [one] wants to be free. It is perhaps the most natural human desire to give oneself away in love. Anything less frustrates the soul. To any young person who is searching for true freedom with ears to hear, may your Catholic elders speak in one voice: To feel free, find someone to love with all your heart who is capable of loving you in return. And once you have, pour yourself out recklessly, give everything to marriage and family, or to a worthy vocation [like priesthood, another consecrated religious vocation, or service to humanity], and miraculously, your cup will forever overflow. It doesn't make sense, but it's not supposed to. It's only supposed to be true. It is. And it will set you free."[359] One should also consider all of the relationships one has, including family and friends, as a stewardship. One possesses the ability to offer blessings to all in those relationships or to withhold them. The ball is in your court to do good to all and not withhold it if it is within your power to give.

Find and Rejoice in the Good in all of Your Works

One should enjoy the rewards of good labor and conscientious, kind-hearted works, whether enterprise-building works, works of charity, or the works that include the rearing of children in godliness, the generational or family building of estates, the governing of a society, etc. A godly heritage is a blessing and reward from the Lord to one who fears God and keeps His commands.

Although Much Wisdom Brings Sorrow, It's Better to Be Wise Than Ignorant and Foolish

Although wise ones sometimes die as fools do, it is still better to be wise, allowing one to walk in the light of Christ and His Kingdom. Being wise enables one to see how things should be and how far from that standard of wisdom and righteousness things are. That standard of ethics has its source in the Word of

---

[359] Laffin, Peter, The Vows of My Freedom, The Catholic Thing Website, thecatholicthing.org, Wed, April 19, 2023.

God. Your observation of these things is perhaps your invitation to make your contribution to bring life closer to heaven on earth. Possessing the wisdom to see and to direct one's steps prudently in the light is better than stumbling in darkness.

Since wisdom cries out to the simple daily, one should ask God for this wisdom and believe one receives it without doubting.[360] Do not become vexed when righteous men receive the judgment of wicked men, and wicked men receive the desserts of the righteous. We can neither see nor know all that God is doing. Wisdom is good when added to a financial inheritance, and a wise man leaves an inheritance to his grandchildren. A wise heart will know time and judgment, which is what the cardinal virtue of prudence is all about. Ask God for wisdom. Ask Him to open your ears and heart daily for Wisdom as she cries out to the simple. Pray, and ask God and exercise faith that you receive His wisdom daily. As Jesus told his disciples as they were about to go forth preaching and teaching the Kingdom of God, "I will inspire you with wisdom which your adversaries will be unable to resist."[361] Consider praying this prayer in faith often:

God of my fathers, Lord of mercy, you who have made all things by your word and in your wisdom have established man to rule the creatures produced by you, to govern the world in holiness and justice, and to render judgment in integrity of heart: Give me Wisdom, the attendant at your throne, and reject me not from among your children; for I am your servant, the son of your handmaid, a man weak and short-lived and lacking in comprehension of judgment and of laws. Indeed, though one be perfect among the sons of men, if Wisdom, who comes from you, be not with him, he shall be held in no esteem. Now with you is Wisdom, who knows your works and was present when you made the world; who understands what is pleasing in your eyes and what is conformable with your commands. Send her forth from your holy heavens and from your glorious throne dispatch her that she may be with me and work with me, that I may know what is your pleasure. For she knows and understands all things, and will guide me discreetly in my affairs and safeguard me by her glory. Glory to

---

[360] Prov 1:20-33; 8:32-36; James 1:5-6.

[361] Luke 21:15.

the Father, and to the Son, and to the Holy Spirit: as it was in the beginning, is now, and will be for ever. Amen.[362]

Godliness and Contentment Is Great Gain

Better to have one's hand full of goods with the quiet attitude of contentment than to have full hands due to toil based on envy and longing for what one cannot know or have, which Solomon calls "longing for the wind." Solomon is referring to those who long for things they can neither grasp nor possess. Therefore, he instructs one to be happy and content in all one's circumstances. However, if you can better yourself in any way through wisdom and the great gift of diligence, do it.

Companionship Is a Gift in this Life

Better are two than one, and three together can accomplish much and can hardly be defeated. This promotes godly marriages and godly and powerful unity in all things, especially within the Church.

Be Humble to the Voice of Wisdom

Better to be teachable, quiet, diligent, and respectful when it comes to the things of this life and the Kingdom of God than to be an arrogant fool.

---

[362] Wisdom 9:1-6, 9-11.

God Sees All, So Never Be Alarmed at Great Oppression and Evil Trying to Hide from His Gaze

Never panic over negative or threatening world events, as the Kingdom comes in the earth. Remember that the last days are behind us and our best days are ahead. Don't be alarmed when nations oppress other nations, for God has placed other nations in a position to watch over those nations that are oppressing. God has a sovereign check and balance system in play as the Kingdom of God is filling the earth. St. Paul wrote to the Thessalonians that it is a righteous thing for God to repay with tribulation those who trouble you. Many times throughout history, the Kingdom of God has come upon evil nations resulting in their collapse, like that of the Soviet Union in the 1980s. It is not the normal course of Providence for God to allow a wicked oppressive nation to last long, for God, unbeknownst to wicked and manipulative governments, hears the cry of the oppressed and avenges them speedily. God may use one nation to punish or chasten other nations that do not fear Him, and once that chastening is accomplished, God may do away with that punishing nation that has gone too far. Remember that all of the nations together are as nothing before God, and with Satan bound, nothing can stop the advance of the Church or the Son's Kingdom from spreading across the globe.[363] Regarding rulers or governments, it should be remembered that although not the norm of history, one should not fret when fools are occupying a high place of power while the righteous occupy low estates. This unusual scene of events does not last long.

All Must Stand Before the Judgment Seat of Christ the King

Know that the righteous and the wicked will be judged by Jesus Christ, either in this life, or in the next. It will not be well with the wicked. Remember that the Lord takes no delight in the death of the wicked. We pray that God may grant grace upon both the wicked and the righteous so that all repent from sin and believe in God's continuing redemption through Christ Jesus.

---

[363] Ps(s) 2.

A Good Reputation Is as Gold in This Life

Pursue a good name and reputation, be humble to correction and the rebuke of those wiser, and be patient in doing good as a humble servant of Christ in every realm of life.

Do Not Long for the Past

Don't long for the fabled "good ol' days." Stay aware of the present, and consider that God's goodness is being made known and manifest in these days and the days to come. These are the blessed days of the Kingdom of God and of Christ's reign foretold by the prophets. Rejoice in them and live in a state of gladness, hope, and overcoming victory as a result. As Solomon has said, during those days of old, others longed for days further back, or longer ago. This longing for what seemed to be better days for some is vanity and grasping for the wind. Beyond an honorable remembrance of the good of long ago, what has happened is gone forever. Look around and look forward!

Be Neither Overly Righteous Nor Overly Wicked

One should not be overly righteous. Loving God with the whole heart and loving neighbor as oneself is sufficient. Don't add to the Commandments. Obeying them from the heart is sufficient. Do not be overly wicked, either. Seek to live in holiness in the fear of God, without which no man will see God.

Don't Fret Over the Words of Others Against You

You should not give yourself to all the words people say or their peer pressure upon you, lest you hear them cursing you. As Solomon rightly has said, your heart knows that you also cursed others many times.

Work Diligently Without Excessive Care About What Happens When You Pass from this Earth

One should make his contributions to this world in all spheres of life and not become vexed over not being able to know or control what will happen to your works after you pass from this life. Leave what happens afterward with God Himself and commit those things to sober and effectual prayer. Regardless of your circumstances in this life, rejoice in the opportunities to make your contributions, for it is better to be alive than dead. If one is alive, there is hope for today and the future. By determination and God's grace, one can immediately change course by correcting behaviors or strategies. One can repent and labor to restore a tarnished or wrecked life, reputation, family, church, state, or enterprise. Life is sweet and life under the sun is pleasing to the eye. The graveyard is full of those who no longer have a portion in anything under the sun. Their fears, worries, concerns, and work under the sun are gone.

Therefore, if one is alive, do as Solomon said when he exhorted the young and old to banish frustration from the heart, and cast away misery from the body. Youth is transient. Therefore, find joy in all things in this life. As Solomon said: it is better to be a living dog, than a dead lion under the sun.

Young Men and Women Must Put off Anxiety and Put on Joy

A young man should rejoice in his youth and enjoy life with his wife whom he loves all of his days, for this is God's portion for both the man and his wife. As to the cultural mandate, the two should pursue bearing and rearing godly children as a contribution to the Kingdom of God and to the world in general. "Why did God make of the two one flesh? To have a godly offspring."[364] Your children will be your best disciples, and they will bring you uncountable joy in your old age. The world and those unlearned in the Kingdom of God and the power of faith in God will always find reasons to reject God's cultural mandate

---

[364] Mal 2:15.

to build in this life. Reject the world's teaching contrary to faith in God and His Word. Put off anxiety, transform your mind by substituting your thoughts and those of the world's with God's Word, pray for His grace and blessing, and then clothe yourself with love, joy, and peace. And live life with a wife and with as many children as God will give. If God calls you to His ministry, or to celibacy as a priest, then seek to discern this call, and fulfill it by aligning yourself with many godly counselors, good and holy Christian mentors.

Arise and Work Diligently and Wisely Every Day

Whatever one's hands find to do in any area of this life should be done with all of one's strength and mind and to the glory of God. One should not be lazy, whether one is a king or a man in a low estate. When it comes to work, use wisdom and sharpen the ax or any other tool necessary to work more effectively and efficiently, including your mind and capabilities. As you go to your labors, you should commit your way to God, ask for His blessing on the work, and then exercise faith to believe He does indeed bless the work.[365] Work six days a week believing God will bless you. Even if your work requires your labors only five days per week, work something different that sixth day and prosper. Also, diversify your interests and investments in order to mitigate the risk of putting all of your "eggs in one basket" and incurring the risk of losing it all. Begin your work diligently in the morning and continue your works into the evening, for you do not know which of your works or investments will prosper. One or the other may prosper, or, perhaps, both with prosper.

Build with Confident Faith in God to Bless Your Future

Seize the day by working, investing, and building. Have the same mind with respect to a family. Venture a large Christian family if God grants you that. Seek

---

[365] Mark 11:23-24.

to be excellent and fruitful in everything you set your mind and hands to do. Request God's blessing upon everything you set your hand to do daily, including the seemingly small and insignificant things. Do not listen intently to those who speak pessimistically about the future, for no one knows what the future holds. Fear of the future paralyzes most of humanity to not venture forth in faith and build. As one grows older, storm clouds of potential doom will always loom on the horizon, so sow your seed and reap your harvest in faith. Solomon's description of the mantra of those paralyzed by unbelief is "He who observes the wind will not sow, and he who regards the clouds will not reap."[366]

Fearing God and Keeping His Commands is EVERYTHING

The whole of man, his consummate duty, his everything is to fear God and keep His Commandments, which means to receive, acknowledge, and obey His Son as Lord and Savior and live a life of joyful obedience and worship of the King.[367]

Doing these things will give one great resolve to one's vexing observations under the sun. As Solomon exhorted, we resolve to fear God and keep Christ's commands, as well as persevere under pressure. We suffer, if need be, to receive Christ's reward. Thomas á Kempis wrote in the 14th century of the virtues of bearing hardship in life under the sun stating, "But the real test of virtue and deserving of praise is to live at peace with the perverse, or the aggressive and those who contradict us, for this needs a great grace…in this mortal life, our peace consists in the humble bearing of suffering and contradictions, not in being free of them, for we cannot live in this world without adversity. Those who can best suffer will enjoy the most peace, for such persons are masters of themselves, lords of the world, with Christ for their friend, and heaven as their reward."[368]

---

[366] Eccl 11:4.

[367] Eccl 12:13-14.

[368] Thomas á Kempis, Imitation of Christ, pp. 72-73.

David the King said, "Say among the nations, 'The Lord reigns; The world also is firmly established, It shall not be moved; He shall judge the peoples righteously. Let the heavens rejoice, and let the earth be glad...'"[369] Christ Jesus has assigned His shepherds over His people who will lead them to green pastures in this world as the Kingdom of God is coming daily and filling the earth. Each day as the people of God pray that second petition of the Lord's prayer from the heart, great hope should swell within them that every principality and power in heaven, earth, and under the earth is bowing the knee to Christ. So we take comfort and are encouraged and confidently say, "The Lord is my Helper [in time of need], I will not be afraid. What will man do to me?" We are sufficiently equipped in Christ to build in this age of His growing Kingdom on earth.[370]

A Daily Prayer for God's Kingdom to Come.

Our Heavenly Father, may Thy Kingdom come and Thy will be done on earth as it is done in heaven. May Your grace fill our lives, our families, our churches, our cities, states, and nations with your righteousness, peace, and joy in the Holy Spirit. May mankind honor Christ the King, learn of His ways, and obey His commands fervently from the heart. May love and truth abound in every place, especially within the hearts of all of mankind from the largest cities to the most remote tribes. May we see the good and prosperity of the Church in our days and may You endow her ministers and her people to bear forth true witness of the Kingdom of God that all men might believe and be saved. May the Word of the Lord roar forth from Zion, and may the Spirit of the Lord work in the hearts of the people of the world to come to the Mountain of the Lord's House to hear His Words and to obey them. May we see peace among nations and the ceasing of warfare. May your Kingdom come in our families and in the lives of all our children that will come from our covenant families. May no one

---

[369] Ps(s) 96:10-11.

[370] Heb 13:5 from the Amplified Bible is particularly edifying: "I will never [under any circumstances] desert you [nor give you up nor leave you without support, nor will I in any degree leave you helpless], nor will I forsake or let you down or relax My hold on you [assuredly not]!"

be lost from our family lines now through the end of time. May there always be members of our family declaring with a full heart of assurance that Christ Jesus reigns, and His Kingdom rules over all. We thank you, Lord, and we believe we receive this answer for it is Your will to save your Church and Your people forever. In the name of the reigning King, Jesus Christ, we pray. Amen.

I close with powerful words that Pope Sixtus V had engraved on the obelisk which stands in the center of Saint Peter's Square at Rome. These magnificent words are in the present tense, and not in the past, to indicate that Christ's triumph is always actual, and that it is brought about in the Eucharist and by the Eucharist:[371]

Christus vincit, regnat, imperat: ab omni malo plemem suam defendat. (Christ conquers, He reigns, He commands; may He defend His people from all evil.)

Now, arise, stand straight and boldly in Christ, be of good cheer, fear not, and continue building!

---

[371] Catholicism Pure & Simple, https://catholicismpure.wordpress.com/2014/04/21/christus-vincit-christus-regnat-christus-imperat/

LISTING OF SOURCES

Beale, G.K.

The Book of Revelation,
New International Greek
Testament Commentary

Boettner, Loraine

The Millennium

Chilton, David

Paradise Restored

Chilton, David

The Days of Vengeance

Chilton, David

The Great Tribulation

Constantinou

Guiding to a Blessed End

Edersheim, Alfred

Life and Times of Jesus the Messiah

Flavius Josephus

The Wars of the Jews

Gentry, Kenneth

He Shall Have Dominion

Gentry, Kenneth

The Beast of the Revelation

Guthrie, Donald

Introduction, New Testament

Hendrikson, William

More Than Conquerors

Kik, J. Marcellus

An Eschatology of Victory

Mounce

The Book of Revelation,
New International Commentary of the
New Testament

Newton, Bishop Thomas

The Prophecy of Matthew 24

Nisbett, N.

The Prophecy of the Destruction
of Jerusalem

Rushdoony, R.J.   Thy Kingdom Come: Studies
                                  in Daniel and Revelation

Russell, James Stuart   The Parousia

Sandlin, Andrew   A Postmillennial Primer

Schaff, Philip   History of the Christian
                                  Church, Volume 1

Williamson, Peter   Revelation

Ignatius Catholic Study Bible of the New Testament

Ladd, George Eldon   Commentary on the Revelation
                                  of John

The Navarre Bible, New Testament

United States Conference of Catholic Bishops, Website, Commentary Notes
on Revelation

Catechism of the Catholic Church   Article 12, I believe in the
                                    Life Everlasting

Biblical Citations: All biblical references are cited from the Holy Bible, New King James Version, BibleGateway, https://www.biblegateway.com/.